PRAISE FOR
RENT ESTATE REVOLUTION

"Renters Warehouse has written the primer for anyone considering real estate investing. A must-read book for beginners—and you learn from the best!"

—SEAN HANNITY, Nationally Syndicated TV and Radio Host, Best-Selling Author, and Real Estate Entrepreneur

"If financial freedom and a secure retirement are your goals, this book will outline the single greatest wealth-creation tool used by the wealthiest people today."

—DARREN HARDY, Founding Publisher/Editor of *SUCCESS, New York Times* Best-Selling Author, and CEO Mentor

"Everybody has a right to invest in real estate, and since barriers to less-experienced investors are lifting, there's a need to educate and inform newcomers. *Rent Estate Revolution* does just that. It's a must-read for anyone starting out down this new path."

—GARY BEASLEY, Co-Founder and CEO of Roofstock

"With a focus on long-term income investing, *Rent Estate Revolution* demystifies real estate investing and speaks to those who are willing to learn, grow, and do what others won't."

—CLAYTON COLLINS, President and CEO of HousingWire

"If you're looking for a well-written, easy-to-read, practical-yet-informative guide on rental investing, this book is it. Ortner and his company continue to redefine and revolutionize Rent Estate, and inspire the entrepreneur in all of us."

—**BETH O'BRIEN,** President and CEO
of Colony American Finance

"Rent Estate Revolution is an outstanding contribution to our developing single-family rental (SFR) industry. I'm especially struck by Ortner's emphasis on the win-win-win nature of SFR. Investors, tenants, and communities all gain when passionate, responsible people invest their time, energy, and money upgrading America's neighborhoods."

—**ED RENWICK,** CEO of Raineth Housing

"Social, demographic, and economic trends continue to shift in support of rentership, and this book is a great resource for anyone seeking information to make better-informed decisions about the properties they're investing in."

—**DENNIS CISTERNA,** Chief Revenue Officer
of Investability Real Estate, Inc.

"The residential real estate market is the entrepreneurial playground for this generation, and Ortner understands how entrepreneurs at all levels can create something incredibly valuable using their own creativity and ingenuity."

—**GREG RAND,** Founder and CEO of OwnAmerica

"This book is a testament to the capital opportunity of the rental economy."

—**SHAWN MILLER,** CEO of 5 Arch Funding

"Renters Warehouse has contributed to my financial success by providing expert advice, operational efficiency, and diligent work—all at a reasonable price. Since my initial work with the company in 2010, I've been extremely satisfied and have recommended them to several friends."

—**GARY BRAUCH,** Rent Estate Investor

"A superb read for anyone who wants the right information on how to make well-informed decisions about the homes they're buying, renting out, and managing."

—**ANDY MELVIN,** Managing Director of IMN

"For anyone building a single-family rental portfolio, *Rent Estate Revolution* is a must-read! Ortner's book should be a reference guide for every investor."

—**EDDIE WILSON,** President of Think Realty

"There's no better way to build wealth than with rental properties, but too many real estate investors and property owners try to manage properties themselves to save money, which is insane. As Ortner points out throughout *Rent Estate Revolution*, if you don't want your Rent Estate investments to age you prematurely, then leave property management to the pros."

—**MIKE HAMBRIGHT,** Chief Nerd at FlipNerd.com

"Investing in the right real estate can be a game-changer for your family's financial future—and today, the right real estate is Rent Estate."

—**JASON WALGRAVE,** Rent Estate Investor

"Rent Estate is freedom. Once we arrived in the Florida Keys, we quickly realized what living a dream felt like: boating, fishing, scuba-diving with the sharks, snorkeling with the turtles, paddle-boarding, and watching every beautiful sunset together as a family. Rent Estate made living in paradise possible."

—**J.D. DICKERSON,** Rent Estate Investor

"Whether you're a seasoned investor or just thinking about dipping your toe into real estate, *Rent Estate Revolution* is an excellent read for anyone. There's more to investing and retirement than stocks and bonds, and Ortner does an excellent job explaining why owning rental properties is a smart long-term investment strategy."

—**JUSTIN COOPER,** Pine Financial Group

RENT ESTATE™ REVOLUTION

RENT ESTATE™
REVOLUTION

Today's Key to Retirement Security, Financial Freedom & the New American Dream

KEVIN ORTNER

Published by SFR Group.

For ordering information or special discounts for bulk purchases, please email sales@RentEstateRevolution.com or visit www.RentEstateRevolution.com.

Cover design by Media Bridge Advertising.

Composition and editing by Accelerate Media Partners, LLC.

Paperback ISBN: 978-0-9988800-1-3
Hardcover ISBN: 978-0-9988800-0-6
EPUB ISBN: 978-0-9988800-2-0
Kindle ISBN: 978-0-9988800-3-7

Library of Congress Control Number: 2017938248

Printed in the United States of America.

To the entire Renters Warehouse team. It's easy to write about Rent Estate. It's harder to make it work behind the scenes—and make it look easy in the process. As someone who spent years on the front lines, I know what it's like to be a grinder. And I'm forever grateful for your hard work and tireless commitment.

CONTENTS

USEFUL RENT ESTATE TERMS

Rent Estate
> An investment tool that involves buying single-family homes to rent to long-term tenants.

Rent Estate Revolution
> The wealth-creation movement in which ordinary Americans are achieving financial freedom and retirement security by investing in single-family homes as rental properties.

Rent Estate Entrepreneur
> Anyone who joins the Rent Estate Revolution.

Renter Nation
> The growing community of people who either invest in or rent residential real estate.

Rent Estate Advisor
> A designation developed by Renters Warehouse to indicate a real estate or other property agent who is well versed in the nuances of finding, financing, and managing single-family properties to rent.

Rent Estate Property
> A residential rental property with one to four units. Also known as a single-family rental, or SFR.

Property Management
> Everything involved in managing a single-family rental property, including collecting rent, managing maintenance requests, and handling paperwork and other red tape.

FOREWORD

by Arthur B. Laffer, PhD
Economic Policy Advisor to President Ronald Reagan

In my half-century as an economist, I've seen my share of trends, patterns, and cycles. Sometimes too much attention is paid to passing fads. Other times, significant changes go too long ignored. *Rent Estate Revolution* gets it exactly right by identifying a development that is new, growing, and poised to have significant staying power in the American economy.

As someone who has studied tax policy for most of his life, I especially appreciate the tax benefits of investments in single-family rentals. The climate is right to provide a low barrier to entry in securing capital, and the significant tax savings of Rent Estate encourage additional investment—which is exactly the kind of productive economic engine we need.

Rent Estate Revolution covers a great deal of ground in an area that can often be complex, but readers will be grateful to find that the book reads nothing like an academic paper. The points are practical and accessible regardless of whether you have a real estate background or a PhD in Economics, yet it respects the reader enough to resist the urge to "dumb things down."

I'm often identified with curves, and author Kevin Ortner is clearly way ahead of the curve on this one. Renting is indeed the new owning for millions of people. And for ordinary investors, Rent Estate represents a significant opportunity that should not be ignored.

—*Dr. Arthur B. Laffer*

WHAT TO EXPECT WITH THIS BOOK

My goal with *Rent Estate Revolution* is simple: I want to help you achieve financial freedom. To do that, we're going to have a conversation in which I open your eyes to the amazing new opportunity called "Rent Estate," and hopefully inspire you to take advantage of it. We'll have this discussion in three parts:

1. We'll learn what Rent Estate is and why the Rent Estate Revolution is here to stay.
2. We'll lay out what's involved in Rent Estate.
3. We'll talk about how to become a Rent Estate Entrepreneur.

To demonstrate how Rent Estate is "real estate for the rest of us," I'll also show you how you can take an initial investment of just $5,000 and grow it into a financial freedom machine fed by other people's money and the cash that Rent Estate generates on its own. Along the way, I'll address some common questions, show you why Rent Estate is so much easier than trying to do property management on your own, and give you a specific action item at the end of every chapter.

Before you dive in, I want you to consider two things: 1) Rent Estate is about *creative leverage*: It's the only investment you can get a bank to finance and a stranger to repay; and 2) Rent Estate isn't really Rent Estate unless you outsource the headache of property management, and that's never been easier.

A final point: It's no secret that I'm the CEO of Renters Warehouse, the nation's largest residential property management company. For the most part, I'm going to pretend that I'm not biased when it comes to outsourcing property management. But along the way, I might mention my company and direct you to some of our excellent Rent Estate eTools. So if I come across a little sales-pitchy, forgive me in advance.

—Kevin Ortner
May 2017

ACKNoWLEDGMENTS

My journey, and subsequently this book, would not have been possible without the early vision of Renters Warehouse founder Brenton Hayden. His reinvention of the property management industry is still the foundation of our business today. Brenton gave me the chance of a lifetime when he bet on a laid-off pilot to help him build this business and change the world. For that, I am forever grateful. Thank you, Brenton.

I also must give thanks to my early business partner, Donovan Reese, and to my brother, Jonathan Ortner. They've been with me nearly every step of the way for almost a decade, and my success wouldn't be possible without them. And to my parents: Thanks for encouraging my first foray into Rent Estate, and for instilling a work ethic that benefits me to this day.

A special thanks to my book-writing team. To the great writing and editing skills of Marc Conklin; the creative, marketing, and editing talent of Pam Kosanke; the professional book publishing team of Reed Bilbray, Ivy Hughes, and Erica Jennings; and to the many, many close colleagues and personal friends who contributed to this project with their time, energy, and stories.

Last, but certainly not least, I'd like to thank my wonderful wife, Tiffany, who for one reason or another continues to put up with my crazy ideas and determination to share the power of Rent Estate with the world. Thank you for always being by my side.

INTRODUCTION

Imagine this.

You recently persuaded your family to move halfway across the country for your job. You've just arrived in your new city and bought a new house while your old one sits on the market. Your wife is looking for a job. Your daughter is trying to make friends at school. And after all this transition, you walk into work one day only to be told that your employer is bankrupt and you've been laid off.

To summarize: At 7:59 A.M., you were still embarking on an exciting new adventure. By 8:00 A.M., you and your spouse are unemployed, with a child to support and two mortgages to pay. Oh, and by the way, it's also the middle of the Great Recession, so the only thing harder than finding a new job is selling a house.

I don't have to imagine this scenario, because I lived it. In May 2009, I was working as a private commercial pilot for a Minnesota-based company. I had just moved my family from Phoenix to the Twin Cities, and the day after we closed on our new house, the rug got pulled out from under us.

It was a nightmare scenario, but here's the surprising thing: I didn't panic. In fact, I actually felt an odd sense of clarity and optimism. Why? Because ever since I was a teenager, I had been devising backup plans in life. Now "Plan B" was about to become "Plan A." My job was about to become my mission. And a new industry was about to become my life's passion—even though it didn't even have a name yet.

Without realizing it, I had actually started my backup plans soon after arriving at Arizona State University in the fall of 2002. Even though I was a fresh-faced college student, I wasn't exactly born with a silver spoon in my mouth. My dad was a cop who built houses on the side (and sometimes employed his kids as cheap labor). He had come from a poor family, so we were raised in the religion of "personal responsibility": Take care of yourself and your family. Don't get entitled. And never expect anyone to bail you out.

I always knew the value of a dollar, and I'd always had an entrepreneurial streak. So when I looked into the Phoenix/Tempe housing market, an idea came to me that I soon presented to my dad: "Help me buy a duplex near campus, and I'll live rent-free in one unit by renting out the other." My dad is a smart guy, so he took me up on the offer. It wasn't a huge "ask"—about $3,000 and a co-sign on the loan—but he had no idea how much that decision would impact me for years to come.

Frankly, neither did I. At the time, I was just trying to save a buck. But after I moved in, got some renters, and crunched the numbers, I realized that this modest little building could deliver more than just four years of free housing. Not only did my tenants cover my mortgage, property taxes, and other expenses; their rent put an extra $150 in my pocket every month. I was studying business at the time (aviation management), and I couldn't help but realize that I was also running a small business. I controlled an asset that was primed to rise in value. Someone else was shelling out the cash to help me own more of it every month. And on top of all that, I was going to clear about $2,000 a year in profit. I wasn't going to be a millionaire overnight, but I definitely wanted to buy more residential real estate properties in the future.

After graduating, I started flying corporate jets. Being a pilot turned out to be the perfect career to support my real estate hobby. With stretches of days or weeks on the ground, I would research other investment properties and add more to my portfolio. I found that I wasn't interested in the high-risk "buy and flip" world. Despite a booming real estate market in the pre-bust years—fueled by banks that were practically giving away money at the time—I was more methodical and conservative by nature. I always went for traditional 30-year terms rather than adjustable or interest-only loans. And despite the constant temptation to buy homes that *might* double in value tomorrow, I favored properties that would gradually appreciate over the long haul.

As I immersed myself in the day-to-day operations of owning multiple rental properties, a life-changing realization hit me: The hardest part isn't locating or financing properties; it's *managing* them. It's finding good tenants, collecting the rent, and handling the maintenance requests. College students would be chronically late with their rent, and then send me checks covering their individual parts of it. I'd get maintenance requests while I was out on a week of flying assignments, so I'd let them sit for days or even months. It was a big headache.

The solution seemed simple: Hire a property management company. But when I looked into it, I was shocked to discover just how disorganized and unprofessional the industry was. No one packaged their services in a logical, efficient, and truly affordable way. Since real estate is such a local business, most property managers were mom-and-pop operations—like those neighborhood video rental places that existed before Blockbuster and Netflix came along.

As I continued to fly all over the country, I couldn't help but think about how much residential property management could be improved. So it was either fate, coincidence, or a little bit of both when I met Brenton Hayden in 2008. Brenton had just started a company called Renters Warehouse in Minnesota, and although it had fewer than 200 properties under management at the time, I immediately fell in love with Brenton's vision: a national, one-stop shop with specialized departments for finding tenants, collecting rent, and managing maintenance. It was exactly what the industry needed.

I don't normally recommend going into business with someone after knowing them for only 45 minutes, but that's exactly what happened with Brenton and me. By the end of one breakfast, I had agreed to invest in the business and open the first Renters Warehouse branch office in Phoenix.

By January 2009, my two careers were locked in a fierce tug of war. As I tried to start a family, fly planes for a company located 1,500 miles away from home, and launch Renters Warehouse Phoenix, I was also getting a serious lesson in multisite property management. One minute I'd be fixing a sink; the next, I'd be banging on a door all the way across town to collect rent (I probably drove more miles than I flew). By spring, I decided that we needed to move up north to be closer to my aviation employer, even if it meant that my second life as a property management entrepreneur would have to take a back seat.

Then May came, the layoff happened, and everything went poof. But instead of freaking out, I felt like everything I had done in real estate suddenly made sense: Buying that duplex in college. Investing in additional properties. Building equity and earning passive income to supplement my salary. Learning the challenges of being a landlord firsthand. Then joining Renters Warehouse and seeing the big picture of property management.

Connecting those dots kept me from panicking. My decisions now shielded me from financial hardship, but they also gave me the chance to accomplish more. I realized that if I kept acquiring more rental properties, I could actually open the doors to financial freedom and retirement security for my family. This fit my upbringing and values perfectly, because frankly, I had never counted on Social Security for much. This was a way to truly take control of my financial future, and I was eager to do it.

When I took a step back, I realized that I was actually part of a Revolution in real estate that was just beginning to gain traction. Dozens of cultural, social, and economic factors were converging: the recession, changing attitudes about homeownership, a desire for greater mobility, traditional investment tools stagnating or failing. The real estate world was changing, and all signs pointed to *renting*.

At Renters Warehouse, we call this the Rent Estate™ Revolution. Rent Estate isn't about buying and renting time-shares, apartment buildings, or vacation properties. And it's not Airbnb'ing your condo during big conventions and sporting events. It's about buying and holding properties to rent to long-term tenants. That's a unique niche, and it's different from traditional real estate.

Rent Estate taps into the growing popularity of single-family rentals, and it uses today's amazing tools to find, purchase, and *manage* those properties. I emphasize "manage" because that's the piece that's been missing until recently. Locating and purchasing a single-family rental has always been doable, but the management element is now so easy and so affordable, you're almost crazy to do it yourself.

Based on my experience, there's no better way to feel good about your financial future than by becoming a Rent Estate Entrepreneur. It's a smart investment, but it also benefits everyone involved. Frankly, some sectors of real estate exploit other people's misfortunes. But Rent Estate helps investors *and* renters—the family who owns the property, as well as the family who lives in it. I've seen Rent Estate provide relief to seniors, repair tenant credit, and strengthen entire cities by keeping urban neighborhoods vibrant and alive. On every financial and emotional level, it's a win-win for all involved.

Much has changed for me since those college days of 2002. I still work for Renters Warehouse, and we're now the largest player in our space. But more importantly, not a day goes by that I don't think about what Rent Estate has done (and continues to do) for me and my family. My wife, Tiffany, and I are now the proud parents of two children and 13 residential properties, including that original duplex in Phoenix. Rent Estate saved us from financial hardship in the past; now it provides a strong source of funding for everything from college tuition to retirement.

We feel a greater sense of financial security than we ever thought possible, because we know that our properties, tenants, financing partners, and property management teams are solid, resilient, and built for the long haul. Best of all, we wake up every morning knowing that we're helping other people realize the same benefits that Rent Estate has delivered to us.

At a time when we seem to be losing the American Dream, I've come to believe that joining the Rent Estate Revolution is the best way for ordinary Americans to get it back. Writing this book may not be the smartest move for me business-wise—after all, I'm revealing the "big secret" and probably inspiring more competition. But that's fine with me. I believe in capitalism, innovation, and the free market. So I say, "Bring it on!"

After you read *Rent Estate Revolution*, I hope you'll feel as passionately as I do about the power of Rent Estate. More important, I hope you'll take *action*. Remember: This isn't your grandfather's real estate; it's something new and different. And it's not limited to the elites; it's "real estate for the rest of us."

Rent Estate is exciting. It's accessible. It's here to stay.

And trust me: If I can do it, then so can you.

SECTION I

THE RENT ESTATE

REVOLUTION

You should really buy some property.

As we begin this flight to your Rent Estate future, that's the 30,000-foot view I want you to see (once a pilot, always a pilot). But my reasons are different from the ones you typically find in those *"buy, flip, and get rich quick!"* real estate books. That's because Rent Estate is the new real estate. It's different. It's not "buy and flip"; it's "buy and hold"—a long-term strategy that helps you weather the storms on your way to a successful landing.

I know Rent Estate personally. I've lived it, I've seen its benefits, and I'm convinced that if you do it right, it has the potential to deliver amazing financial benefits right to your doorstep—even if you're not exactly made of money right now.

Whether you're a Millennial, Gen Xer, or Baby Boomer, there's something in Rent Estate for *you*. Looking for a little extra cash every month? Check. Want to broaden your retirement portfolio? Check. Seeking ways to fund your kids' college education? Check. Looking for an investment path that might let you quit your day job and do the things you really love to do? Check.

Rent Estate truly is a Revolution, but I get it: "revolution" can be an overused word. When big changes come to society—be they technological, cultural, or economic—it's hard to know when to trust their staying power. After all, the chairman of IBM once said he thought there was a market for only five home computers (in 1943), and an executive at 20th Century Fox famously predicted that TV would fade away after six months.[1]

You may have the same skepticism about Rent Estate, but I don't. I think it's a fundamental movement in our society, and I want you to take advantage of it *now*. The chapters in this section come down

---

1 Robert Strohmeyer, "The 7 Worst Tech Predictions of All Time," *PC World*, December 31, 2008, http://www.pcworld.com/article/155984/worst_tech_predictions.html.

to one point: Rent Estate is a "thing," and it's here to stay. But you be the judge. If you're not swayed after I make my case, feel free to close this book and ignore the Rent Estate Revolution happening all around you.

After all, that'll leave more property for the rest of us.

CHAPTER 1

THE RENT ESTATE EVOLUTION

Rent Estate is the present and the future. But before we dive into that, let's touch quickly on the past. Because to understand the truc power of Rent Estate, you need to go back to the moment when it was born: the Great Recession.

> **"When it comes to real estate, an old system has burned away and allowed a new one to take root that's stronger, more fertile, and better able to thrive."**

The fact is, the farther we get from those gloomy days of 2007–09, the easier it is to forget the impact it had on ordinary Americans. Luckily, most of the negative effects have eased as the economy has recovered. Some stubbornly remain, though, and unfortunately, many people still suffer. Other aspects of the fallout have been helpful—like a forest fire that destroys old trees but spurs newer, more vibrant growth. When it comes to real estate, an old system has burned away and allowed a new one to take root that's stronger, more fertile, and better able to thrive.

To be sure, the Great Recession's devastation is hard to underestimate.

Consider these three facts:

- **8.7 million** Americans lost their jobs.[1]

- More than **9.3 million** Americans went through a foreclosure, lost their home to a lender, or sold their home via a distress sale.[2]

- The total value of real estate owned by U.S. households fell by **$6 trillion**.[3]

Look at those numbers again. Millions out of work and out of their homes. Trillions in wealth flying out the window. The American Dream of a safe and secure retirement gone overnight.

These are crushing statistics. But more important, they reflect the financial and emotional stress we all had to endure when the housing bubble burst. Millions of families had poured their blood, sweat, tears, and life savings into owning their homes. Then, in the blink of an eye, it all disappeared.

Imagine that. You wake up and suddenly can't make your mortgage payment. You owe more on your home than it's worth. And even if you put a For Sale sign in your front yard, no one notices or cares. Maybe you don't have to imagine it. Maybe you were one of the millions of people who lived through it—who felt completely stuck and like there was no way out.

Luckily, there *was* a way out, even if people didn't see it right away. Because a funny thing happened after the housing bubble burst: Rather than walking away from their mortgages or going through

---

1 "Chart Book: The Legacy of the Great Recession," Center on Budget and Policy Priorities, March 10, 2017, http://www.cbpp.org/research/economy/chart-book-the-legacy-of-the-great-recession.

2 Laura Kusisto, "Many Who Lost Homes to Foreclosure in Last Decade Won't Return," *Wall Street Journal*, April 20, 2015, https://www.wsj.com/articles/many-who-lost-homes-to-foreclosure-in-last-decade-wont-return-nar-1429548640.

3 Amir Sufi and Atif Mian, "Why the Housing Bubble Tanked the Economy and the Tech Bubble Didn't," FiveThirtyEight, May 12, 2014, https://fivethirtyeight.com/features/why-the-housing-bubble-tanked-the-economy-and-the-tech-bubble-didnt/.

the pain of foreclosure, some people decided to rent out their homes instead. Most of them didn't really have a choice. But as they soon found out, even though the market for home *buyers* was weak, the demand for home *renters* was surprisingly strong. Why?

The Great Recession was actually conjuring a perfect storm that would give birth to the Rent Estate Revolution. This storm consisted of three major parts:

- Millions of Millennials were emerging from college, saddled with huge debts and unable to afford a home.
- More and more people weren't interested in owning a home and being tied down to any single job or location.
- The number of single-family homes available for rent was exploding due to many homeowners being "underwater" (owing more on their homes than the homes were worth).

Note the mix of economic and cultural factors at play here. Millions of people who couldn't sell their homes joined forces with millions of others who couldn't afford to buy one. At the same time, a younger population was coming of age who wanted things on demand and with no commitments—the same people who would soon embrace Uber, Airbnb, and the entire Sharing Economy. This group was also unique in another important way: They were waiting longer than any generation in history to get married and start a family.

Putting all of this together produced an ideal environment for change, and that's exactly what happened. The perfect storm doused the fires of the Great Recession, and the ground became ripe for a new forest to grow.

As the Great Recession eased, most things—like employment and consumer spending—returned to normal. But real estate and home-ownership changed forever. First, the people who rented single-family homes realized that they liked the freedom and mobility that it provided. Second, the people who rented out those homes stumbled on the same discovery that I made at Arizona State in 2002: Not only could they cover their mortgages, taxes, and other expenses with their rental payments, but they could even clear a small profit every month.

Suddenly, millions of people grasped something that has actually been true for centuries. It's the same thing I described in the introduction to *Rent Estate Revolution*: If you own a home, you own a business. And if you run that business right, you can make a lot of money over time.

Today, Rent Estate continues to gain momentum because it's fueled by something that has always stood at the heart of the American way of life: *freedom*. For tenants, renting offers freedom from mortgages and feelings of being "tied down." For homeowners, Rent Estate opens the doors to financial freedom. It starts by giving you a chance to make a small profit every month on a single asset. Properly grown and managed, it can add a rich slice to your retirement pie—eventually empowering you to quit your day job and achieve a lifestyle you never thought possible.

SINGLE-FAMILY HOMES AND THE RENTAL MARKET
Share of Single-Family Homes That Are Rented

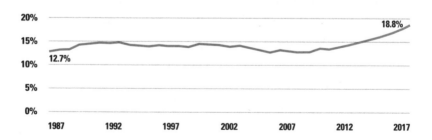

Source: Zillow analysis of U.S. Census Bureau, Current Population Survey, March Supplement, 1979-2015, made available by the University of Minnesota, IPUMS-USA.

This all sounds great. But as with any big economic shift, the key to taking advantage of it is jumping in early. Nearly 10 years after the birth of Rent Estate, I'm convinced that its full power has barely

RENTING HAS SURGED OVER THE PAST SEVERAL YEARS AS HOMEOWNERSHIP HAS STALLED

Average Annual Growth in Households (Millions)

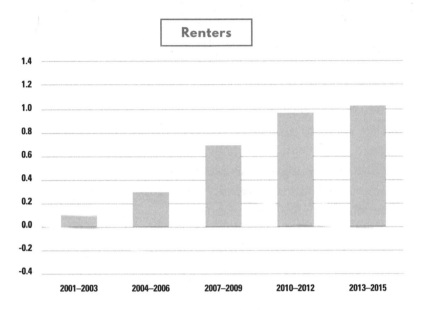

Renters

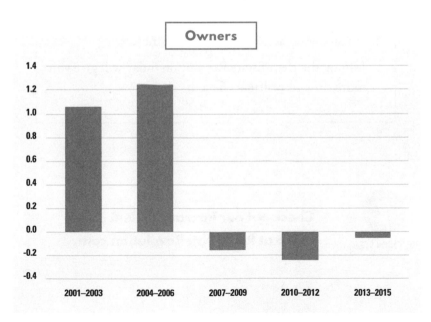

Owners

Source: JCHS tabulations of US Census Bureau, Housing Vacancy Surveys.

been tapped. In other words, the sooner you join the Rent Estate Revolution, the better off you'll be.

So let's jump in.

RENT ESTATE RECAP

The Great Recession burned down old attitudes about real estate and cultivated a new and more fertile landscape: Rent Estate. Every day, more individuals, couples, and families realize that renting a single-family home is actually preferable to buying. And more investors realize that buying homes to rent out is a smart financial move.

---

3 TAKEAWAYS

1. Renting is the new owning, and Rent Estate is the new real estate.

2. If you own a home, you own a business.

3. Joining the Rent Estate Revolution today will give you more time to realize its benefits tomorrow.

ACTION ITEM

Check out our interactive Rent Estate video at RentEstateRevolution.com.

CHAPTER 2

WHY RENT ESTATE IS HERE TO STAY

Gary was in his 60s when he rented out his home in California and moved to Minnesota to be closer to his grandkids. He wasn't comfortable with his retirement savings relying solely on the stock market, so he decided that he needed to add to the pot while diversifying his portfolio. When Gary got to the Twin Cities, he bought a very affordable townhouse, then rented it out and started clearing so much in profit (about $700/month) that he was able to buy three more properties and rent them out as well.

Now Gary is so happy about what Rent Estate has done for him that he's introduced it to his Gen X son: Each time his son has to move for his job, he rents his previous residence instead of selling it. And thus, retirement security through Rent Estate is being handed down from one generation to the next.

This example shows the real power of Rent Estate and begs the question: How deep are the roots of this new movement, and does it offer something for the *many*, or just the elite few? If you're starting to consider Rent Estate as an investment opportunity, then your inner skeptic is probably asking these and many more questions. Since I can't sit down with each one of you over coffee or a beer, I'm going to voice these typical concerns (and hopefully answer them) with a feature I call "The Skeptic Speaks."

"Is Rent Estate truly a 'revolution,' or more just a fad? And is it relevant to all generations?"

It's good to be skeptical (ask anyone who decided *not* to bet on the success of Betamax, BlackBerry, or Google Glass). But here's the thing about Rent Estate: As you're about to see, economic and demographic trends overwhelmingly point to its stability, longevity, economic power, and relevance across generations.

What follows is a snapshot of what Rent Estate really looks like. Bottom line: Renter Nation is big, growing, and here to stay. And no matter which generation you belong to, there's almost certainly a place in it for you.

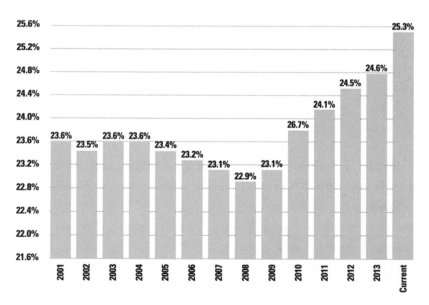

RENTS ARE SOARING
Rents as a Percentage of Median Income

Year	Percentage
2001	23.6%
2002	23.5%
2003	23.6%
2004	23.6%
2005	23.4%
2006	23.2%
2007	23.1%
2008	22.9%
2009	23.1%
2010	26.7%
2011	24.1%
2012	24.5%
2013	24.6%
Current	25.3%

Source: John Burns Real Estate Consulting LLC; RealFacts; REIS (April 2015)

Millennials: One Dream Delayed, Another One Realized

Owning a home has always been central to the American Dream. But for many people in my generation (I'm a "senior Millennial"), that dream is being pushed out quite a ways. At the same time, a New American Dream is emerging around Rent Estate. First, what's on the way out. Our dreams of homeownership can be summed up in these two stats:

- American homeownership recently fell to its **lowest level since 1965**, at less than 63%.[1]

- Homeownership rates among Americans under age 35 also recently hit a record low, at just **34.1%**.[2]

DEMOGRAPHICS OF RENTERS WHO ARE SINGLE-FAMILY RENTERS

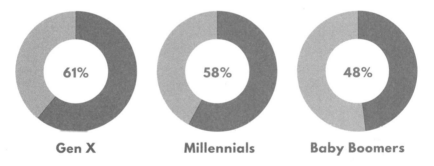

Gen X	Millennials	Baby Boomers
61%	58%	48%

Source: Freddie Mac

Put simply, homeownership is less popular now than it has ever been—especially among Millennials—which has made renting more

---

1   Prashant Gopal, "Homeownership Rate in the U.S. Drops to Lowest Since 1965," Bloomberg, July 28, 2016, https://www.bloomberg.com/news/articles/2016-07-28/homeownership-rate-in-the-u-s-tumbles-to-the-lowest-since-1965.

2   Catherine Rampell, "Millennials Aren't Buying Homes. Good for Them." *Washington Post*, August 22, 2016, https://www.washingtonpost.com/opinions/millennials-arent-buying-homes--good-for-them/2016/08/22/818793be-68a4-11e6-ba32-5a4bf5aad4fa_story.html?utm_term=.eec738f1549f.

popular. There's no sign that either trend is going to reverse itself. In fact, when you look at the people coming into the housing market, the decline is likely to continue. The homeownership rate for young people is just over half of the overall average. And even though you'd expect it to be going up, it's actually going down.[3]

U.S. HOMEOWNERSHIP PERCENTAGE RATE
Homeownership Has Tumbled to 1960s Levels

Source: U.S. Census Bureau

So why is renting beating homeownership, even at a time of relatively low interest rates? Two things: changing economics and changing attitudes. "Location, location, location" has always been the mantra in real estate, but when it comes to choosing a place to live, there's no denying that renting offers more choices and more freedom. Renting gives Millennials the power to live where we can't afford to buy. Plus, when the boiler goes out or the house needs a new roof, it's the landlord's problem, not ours. And Millennials like that. (Who doesn't?)

---

3   Ibid.

Research on Millennials points to the fact that we care more about *experiences* than ownership[4]. If I want to go to a concert, I don't care if I own the car that gets me there. It's just a means to an end. Similarly, if I want to live in that cool new part of the Warehouse District (nearly every city seems to have one), then I don't care if I own the four walls around me. I just want to be there. That's a dramatic shift from the era when a car symbolized "freedom" and a mortgage equaled "stability." And do you think the generations after mine—the ones raised on Snapchat, virtual reality, and self-driving cars—are going to revert to being *more* traditional? Not likely.

So culture and lifestyle are powerful forces in the growing popularity of renting. But let's get real: The biggest factors are economic. Rising home prices and stagnant wage growth are pricing Millennials out of the market. Banks have raised lending standards and made it harder to secure financing, even with low interest rates. If you're a college grad with student loan debt, it now takes about 10 years to save up for a down payment on a house. If you're a non-college-graduate, it takes five years more.[5] When it comes to owning a home, Millennials are simply less interested and less able to do it than previous generations—especially if we don't have access to the First National Bank of Mom & Dad.

But here's the thing: If you're a Millennial like me, this push on the "demand" side of the equation stands to benefit us on the "supply" side. In other words, because so many people in our generation are renting, we're in the best position to meet their needs and make money in the process.

As we'll explore in the chapters to come, the barriers to acquiring single-family properties are surprisingly low. Remember that duplex I

---

4   Uptin Saiidi, "Millennials Are Prioritizing 'Experiences' Over Stuff," CNBC, May 5, 2016, http://www.cnbc.com/2016/05/05/millennials-are-prioritizing-experiences-over-stuff.html.

5   Andrew Woo, "Is Student Debt Stopping Millennials from Homeownership?" *Apartment List*, May 19, 2016, https://www.apartmentlist.com/rentonomics/student-debt-and-Millennial-homeownership-2016/.

bought in Phoenix as a college student? That required a down payment of only about $3,000. I never had to put more of my own money (or my dad's) into it, and it helped me finance additional properties. That's a clue as to why the younger you are, the easier it is to grow your Rent Estate Empire and achieve long-term financial freedom.

Generation X: Bearing the Brunt, But Catching on Quickly

There's good reason why Generation X has been dubbed "one of the most challenged generations of the 20th century" when it comes to homeownership.[6] But if you're a Gen Xer, you're also in a great position to capitalize on Rent Estate if you act quickly.

First, the challenges. Millennials were relatively young when the recession hit, and Baby Boomers had acquired some equity to cushion the blow. But many Gen Xers bought their first home right before the housing bubble burst—so when prices went off the cliff, so did their finances. Millions were left with little or no equity, went underwater, or faced foreclosure.

Now that we're a decade on and Gen Xers have reached middle age, you would expect them to have recovered. But they haven't. Homeownership rates among Gen Xers have fallen further than those of any other generation, and stand 4–5 percentage points lower than they were just 20 years ago.[7] Nearly 20 million current renters used to be homeowners. About a quarter lost their homes to foreclosure during the housing crisis. And most are middled-aged Gen Xers.[8] Translation: While millions of Gen Xers who used to own homes are now renting for lifestyle reasons, for millions of others, it's purely

---

6   Neal Pollock, "Gen X? Good Luck Buying a House—You'll Need It," Realtor.com, August 14, 2015, http://www.realtor.com/news/trends/why-gen-x-is-the-most-screwed-by-the-real-estate-market/.

7   Joint Center for Housing Studies of Harvard University, "The State of the Nation's Housing, 2015," June 24, 2015, http://www.jchs.harvard.edu/sites/jchs.harvard.edu/files/jchs-sonhr-2015-ch1.pdf.

8   Wei Lei, "The Housing Bust Hit Middle-Aged Former Homeowners Hardest," Urban Institute, March 28, 2016, http://www.urban.org/urban-wire/housing-bust-hit-middle-aged-former-homeowners-hardest.

economic. They haven't been able to repair their credit, save money, and buy another home.

FOR A MORE IN-DEPTH LOOK AT RENTING AMONG YOUNGER GENERATIONS, DOWNLOAD "THE HANDBOOK TO WHAT MILLENNIALS WANT" @ RentEstateRevolution.com

But if you're a Gen Xer, you have essentially the same opportunities as Millennials: The need for rental homes is solid and growing, including among people in your own generation. So how can you capitalize on this demand? Simple: Rent Estate. You may not have the same time frame as Millennials to build a Rent Estate portfolio, but you probably have more money available to enter the market—and little or no student debt to deal with. The key is to act quickly.

Baby Boomers: Greater Freedom, Greater Security

You might think that an aging generation like the Baby Boomers would be largely left outside of the Rent Estate Revolution. But as the Gary example illustrates, if you're a Boomer, your peers are already taking advantage of Rent Estate in surprising ways—and so can you.

Our stereotypical images of Baby Boomers are those stock characters from pharmaceutical ads. If it isn't the couple sitting in adjacent bathtubs, it's the grandma in her big suburban house looking grateful for her new reverse mortgage. But when it comes to housing, a growing number of Baby Boomers are bucking the stereotypes and embracing the personal and financial benefits of renting.

If you're a Boomer, you actually have more in common with your Millennial grandkids than you might realize.

Both of you enjoy the freedom of the renter lifestyle—like not having to mow or shovel, and being able to walk to your favorite restaurants and entertainment venues. You also like the freedom of not being tied to a mortgage. And as the share of single-family rentals has surged to a 30-year high,[9] you're responsible for a shocking amount of that growth. According to a study by Harvard University's Joint Center for Housing Studies:

- Between 2005 and 2013, homeownership fell by **5 percentage points** among people 50 to 64.

- In 2005, there were just **10 million renters** in their 50s and 60s. Ten years later, that number grew to **15 million.**

- Baby Boomers are responsible for **more than half** of the nation's renter growth in the last 10 years.[10]

If you're a Boomer, you're renting more than ever due to a mix of lifestyle and economic factors—just like your Millennial and Gen Xer colleagues. Renting frees up more money so you can enjoy retirement on a day-to-day basis (if you're already retired). And, just like your grandkids, you're happy with a lifestyle that trades a little space for a lot of convenience.

But even more interesting is how many of you are becoming Rent Estate investors. As Bloomberg put it in a recent article: "Boomers' New Retirement Plan Is Millennials Paying Rent."[11] People like you are selling their homes, taking the cash from the equity they've built up, renting a smaller place to live in, and buying additional homes to rent out.

That makes perfect sense. No generation has more money to invest. And in a world where Social Security grows more tenuous every day, bonds yield next to nothing, and the stock market remains ever

---

9 Patricia Clark and Suzanne Woolley, "Landlord Nation: Boomers' New Retirement Plan Is Millennials Paying Rent," Bloomberg, August 4, 2016, https://www.bloomberg.com/news/articles/2016-08-04/landlord-nation-boomers-new-retirement-plan-is-millennials-paying-rent.

10 Gail MarksJarvis, "More Older Americans Becoming Renters," *Chicago Tribune*, April 2, 2016, http://www.chicagotribune.com/business/ct-boomer-renters-0403-biz-20160401-story.html.

11 Patricia Clark and Suzanne Woolley, "Landlord Nation: Boomers' New Retirement Plan Is Millennials Paying Rent," Bloomberg, August 4, 2016, https://www.bloomberg.com/news/articles/2016-08-04/landlord-nation-boomers-new-retirement-plan-is-millennials-paying-rent.

volatile, Rent Estate opens up an additional source of income and diversification—offering the hope of greater retirement security.

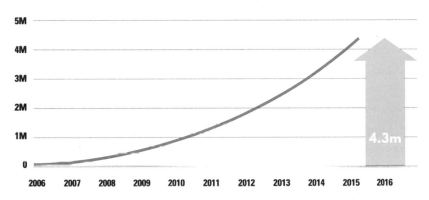

BABY BOOMER RENTERS

Number of Renters Between 50 and 60 Increased by 4.3 Million in the Past 10 Years, with a Decline in Homeownership Rates

Source: TransUnion SmartMove, "State of the U.S. Rental Market in 2016"

The Future

Rent Estate looks like a solid phenomenon right now, but you might be wondering about the next decade and future generations. If so, these projections from the Urban Institute[12] are eye-opening, to say the least:

- Homeownership in the U.S. will continue to **decrease** for at least the next 15 years.

- In the millions of new households forming over the next 15 years, **new renters** will outnumber new homeowners.

- Specifically, **59%** of the 22 million new households that will form between 2010 and 2030 will rent, while just **41%** will buy their homes.

- During that 20-year period, homeownership will **continue to fall** for all age groups under 75.

---

12 Laurie Goodman, Rolf Pendall, and Jun Zhu, "A Lower Homeownership Rate Is the New Normal," *Urban Wire: Housing and Housing Finance*, June 9, 2015, http://www.urban.org/urban-wire/lower-homeownership-rate-new-normal.

Note the frame of reference here. We're not talking about one year, five years, or even a decade from now. We're talking 2030 and beyond. It all adds up to one thing: a surging demand for single-family rentals.

RENT ESTATE REMINDER
The Rent Estate Revolution crosses many generations, and you can benefit no matter where you are in your investment journey.

If you want to know where we're headed, just look at what investors are doing. Optimistic about the future for rental housing, many have been snatching up properties—especially in the single-family market. In the first half of 2016, institutional investors bought 2.9 percent of all single-family homes bought and sold in the U.S. That's up from 2.6 percent the year before (a 12 percent boost), despite rising prices.[13]

So new renters will continue to come on board in waves. But what about the millions of people *currently* renting? Won't they finally start buying homes, and thus negate the newcomers?

Nope. According to a recent Zillow survey,[14] 86 percent of current renters still don't have the income to purchase a home or a high-enough credit score to obtain financing. Nearly half of the survey's participants indicated that they were already spending at least 30 percent of their pre-tax income on rent, making it nearly impossible to qualify for financing on a home. In short: Most renters aren't becoming buyers anytime soon.

---

13 Bendix Anderson, "Institutional Investors Keep Buying Single-Family Rentals, In Spite of High Prices," *National Real Estate Investor,* September 12, 2016, http://nreionline.com/single-family-housing/institutional-investors-keep-buying-single-family-rentals-spite-high-prices.

14 Sean Williams, "R.I.P., Homeownership: It Was Nice Knowing You," *The Motley Fool,* August 21, 2016, http://www.fool.com/investing/2016/08/21/rip-home-ownership-it-was-nice-knowing-you.aspx.

RENT ESTATE RECAP

Renter Nation is widespread and growing. On both the demand side (people renting homes instead of buying them) and the supply side (people buying homes to rent out to other people), Millennials, Gen Xers, and Baby Boomers are all taking part. And it's not just a passing trend. Experts project that renting will continue growing in popularity through at least 2030. So no matter which generation you belong to, it's a good time to join the Rent Estate Revolution.

3 TAKEAWAYS

1. Rent Estate is already delivering financial and lifestyle benefits for people of every generation.

2. The younger you are, the more you can benefit financially from Rent Estate in the long run. The older you are, the easier it is to get started and build your portfolio.

3. Even if you're in your 20s and can only scrape up a few thousand dollars in capital, chances are you can invest in a rental property. And once you have your first property, financing future properties only gets easier.

ACTION ITEM

Download the "Join the Rent Estate Club" infographic at RentEstateRevolution.com to learn why over 22 million people already count themselves as Rent Estate Entrepreneurs.

CHAPTER 3

RENT ESTATE =
FINANCIAL FREEDOM

J.D. Dickerson lived in Houston with his family, working a day job while steadily acquiring single-family homes to rent in the area. After he had over a dozen houses, he realized that he was spending all of his spare time managing properties instead of enjoying his family. And that was an especially big problem, because he had promised his kids that they would take a long "family sabbatical" before they started going off to college.

On J.D.'s 45th birthday, his wife gave him an ultimatum: We do the trip now or never. J.D. did the smart thing. He turned over his property management to us, loaded up the family (including two dogs), and headed down to the Florida Keys. The plan was to return to Houston after one year, but guess what? J.D. and family are still in Florida. Once they experienced their awesome family-first lifestyle, J.D. quit his day job and decided to live off of his Rent Estate income. Instead of constantly finding tenants, collecting rent, and trafficking maintenance requests, he's paddle-boarding, scuba diving, and spearfishing—all while the equity in his properties continues to build his retirement nest egg.

In addition to homeownership, the promise of a secure retirement has long been at the heart of the American Dream. And for decades, people have banked on one thing in particular to fund it: the equity in the home they live in. Well, that's changed. Home and retirement are still connected, but as J.D.'s story illustrates, they're linked in a whole new way. And if you want to take advantage of this new relationship, you need to understand its many nuances.

> "Rent Estate is freedom. Once we arrived in the Keys, we quickly realized what living a dream felt like: boating, fishing, scuba diving with the sharks, snorkeling with the turtles, paddle-boarding, and watching every beautiful sunset together as a family. Rent Estate made living in paradise possible."
>
> —Rent Estate Rockstar, J.D. Dickerson

FOR MORE ON J.D.'S RENT ESTATE JOURNEY, CHECK OUT HIS "RENT ESTATE ROCKSTARS" VIDEO @ RentEstateRevolution.com

First, let's take a moment to talk about the current state of retirement. I believe that we Americans should feel good about the second half of our lives. Instead, most of us are deeply insecure about it. When companies stopped offering pensions, vehicles like 401(k)s and Roth IRAs were supposed to usher in a new, do-it-yourself retirement savings culture. But it isn't working as planned. Many people are struggling, and we need to do something about it—fast.

- **Couples need help.** The median working-age couple has saved only $5,000 for their retirement, and 70% of couples have less than $50,000 saved.[1]

---

1   Rex Nutting, "The Typical American Couple Has Only $5,000 Saved for Retirement," *Market-Watch*, June 15, 2016, http://www.marketwatch.com/story/the-typical-american-couple-has-only-5000-saved-for-retirement-2016-04-28.

- **Millennials need help.** 40% of Millennials say they don't have a retirement strategy in place.[2]

- **Gen Xers need help.** The median savings rate for this group is $70,000, even though most say they'll need $1 million[3] to retire with a similar lifestyle to what they have now.

- **Even Baby Boomers need help.** Average Americans between the ages of 55 and 64 have accrued about $104,000 in retirement savings—an amount that equates to just over $300 a month if invested in a lifetime annuity.[4]

Against these shortfalls, faith in Social Security is also plummeting. A whopping 83 percent of Gen Xers don't expect Social Security to be around when they retire,[5] and for good reason: Most of them will turn 67 a year before Social Security trust funds are projected to run out of money. As for Millennials, a Pew Research survey finds that only 6 percent of them expect current Social Security benefits to be there when they hit 67—and more than half expect them to disappear altogether.[6]

Doom and gloom are easy to find when it comes to Social Security. But whatever happens, the point is this: Even though most Americans don't expect much from Social Security, they also don't currently have the retirement savings they need on their own. So something needs to fill the gap. Enter Rent Estate.

---

2   Sergio Chalbaud, "Millennials Aren't Saving Enough for Retirement. Here's How They Can Fix That," CNBC, September 20, 2016, http://www.cnbc.com/2016/09/20/Millennials-arent-saving-enough-for-retirement-heres-how-they-can-fix-that-commentary.html.

3   Richard Eisenberg, "7 Retirement Mistakes Gen X Is Making," *Forbes*, August 28, 2014, http://www.forbes.com/sites/nextavenue/2014/08/28/7-retirement-mistakes-gen-x-is-making/#3f61bb127391.

4   Tim Parker, "The Average Retirement Savings by Age for 2016," *Investopedia*, December 8, 2016, http://www.investopedia.com/articles/personal-finance/011216/average-retirement-savings-age-2016.asp.

5   Steve Vernon, "Not Too Late for Gen Xers to Save for Retirement," *CBS MoneyWatch*, September 10, 2014, http://www.cbsnews.com/news/not-too-late-for-gen-xers-to-save-for-retirement (9/10/14).

6   Ben Steverman, "Social Security Will Be There for You, Millennials," *Bloomberg*, June 22, 2016, http://www.bloomberg.com/news/articles/2016-06-22/social-security-will-be-there-for-you-millennials.

"What a minute. Are you suggesting that Rent Estate can replace Social Security?"

No, of course not. I'm saying that Rent Estate is potentially *way better*. It's more than a Revolution in real estate. It's more than a smarter way to handle property. And it's more than a solid investment opportunity. When you add it all up, Rent Estate is the best way to achieve financial freedom and retirement security, period.

For me, this goes all the way back to the American Dream and an idea enshrined in our Declaration of Independence: "the pursuit of happiness." The dream hasn't gone away; it's just changed. And the pursuit is still there; there's just a different way to achieve it.

Let's look at shifting views of wealth creation from a personal finance perspective. For decades, the status quo in money management and retirement savings has been the following:

- You buy a home to live in, build up your equity, and assume that you'll sell it around the time you retire.

- Along the way, you hire an accountant for tax advice; an attorney for wills, trusts, and inheritances; and a financial advisor to create a portfolio that consists almost entirely of stocks and bonds. Maybe you start a Roth IRA and a 529 for the kids' college tuition.

- As you work, you squirrel away whatever you can in the company 401(k).

- You hope that all these tools will provide enough of a return to allow you to quit working when you're 65.

In a Rent Estate world, this changes to the following:

- You rent or buy a home to live in, but you also leave the door open for other single-family rentals that you can purchase.

- When you do find a property, you use the power of creative leverage to buy it and pay back the loan.

- You still have a financial advisor, accountant, and attorney. But you also have a Rent Estate Advisor to help you build a significant Rent Estate slice into your financial portfolio pie.

- Eventually, you earn enough passive income from your Rent Estate holdings that you can quit your day job and retire early.

J.D. Dickerson tapped the power of Rent Estate to get exactly what he always wanted out of life. And he was able to do it because Rent Estate offers a unique set of benefits that no other investment—including traditional real estate—can match. I call these benefits:

The Four Pillars of Financial Freedom with Rent Estate

1. Long-Term Cash Flow

2. Equity

3. Appreciation

4. Tax Breaks

The traditional buy-and-sell real estate game can't deliver all of these benefits, but Rent Estate can. We'll get into the math in Chapter 9, "Rent Estate by the Numbers," but here's a broad overview of how each pillar opens the doors to financial freedom for you and your family.

1. Long-Term Cash Flow

What's better than someone else paying your mortgage, plus a little on top? As I realized in college: nothing. And that's what separates Rent Estate from real estate.

Traditional real estate investing is a series of one-and-done transactions, and its success depends too much on luck and timing. You buy a property. You hope the real estate market goes up in that area. You do your best to time the market. And *ding*. Like a slot machine, the coins roll out once, and you're done.

Rent Estate is cumulative and repetitive—like a magic cash register that keeps ringing over and over as long as you want it to. *Ka-ching! Ka-ching! Ka-ching!*

Once you have the right property, you can collect more cash than it takes to own and maintain it. And frankly, that's never been easier to do. Remember all those stats about the popularity of renting and the skyrocketing demand for single-family rentals? Couple that with the fact that rents have been rising faster than inflation in most markets for several years, and you can probably charge a rent that creates positive long-term cash flow right away. As long as the property is occupied, you can ring the cash register.

Remember, this is a long-term strategy. When you clear a couple hundred bucks every month, it definitely adds up.

But even if the rent you collect doesn't completely cover the mortgage, you're still investing in an asset just like you would a 401(k). Plus, while someone else is chipping away at your mortgage, you're the one gaining equity in that property. *Ka-ching!*

2. Equity

Buy-and-flip strategies don't rely on equity. In fact, they ignore it. A traditional real estate mindset obsesses over finding and buying severely undervalued properties for as little as possible, then hoping the market turns around to make them more valuable (on paper) overnight. These "needles in the real estate haystack" are getting harder and harder to find.

Shopping for Rent Estate relies on some of the same principles. You always want to buy properties primed to rise in value. But unlike buy-and-flip real estate, Rent Estate is about building equity. It's just that someone else is doing it for you, hopefully across multiple properties. And the extra beauty of it is this: While your mortgage payment always stays fixed, you have the flexibility to raise the rent when appropriate—and thus accelerate your equity.

As I learned in college: Every time that rent check arrives with someone else's name on it, you own more of your house, and the bank owns less. *Ka-ching!*

3. Appreciation

With Rent Estate, the same principle that applies to equity also applies to appreciation. All real estate relies on the fact that over time, home values go up, and that fact has been proven over and over again. In fact, single-family home prices have consistently risen during every decade since 1940.[7]

But while real estate taps that benefit for only a short time, Rent Estate taps it for the long term. As someone else builds your equity for you, you can also watch the value of your asset rise for 15, 20, even 30 years.

> "After 30 years, you can have a totally paid-for property that—even at a modest appreciation rate—is worth more than twice as much as when you bought it."

In short, real estate treats a home as a temporary asset that you own very little of and (hopefully) sell after a quick burst of appreciation. Rent Estate takes longer but carries a bigger reward: After 30 years, you can have a totally paid-for property that—even at a modest appreciation rate—is worth more than twice as much as when you bought it. Patience is a virtue, right? *Ka-ching!*

---

7   United States Census Bureau, "U.S. Census Single-Family Home Prices Adjusted for Inflation," U.S. Census Bureau, Housing and Household Economic Statistics Division, June 6, 2012, https:// www.census.gov/hhes/www/housing/census/historic/values.html.

4. Tax Breaks

And then there's the IRS (there's always the IRS). Actually, Uncle Sam is on your side when it comes to Rent Estate. With rental properties, you can deduct a whole host of expenses, including the following:

- Management fees
- Maintenance costs
- Advertising
- Depreciation
- Travel
- Mortgage Interest
- Insurance
- Legal and professional fees

EXPENSE BREAKDOWN (SINGLE-FAMILY RENTALS)

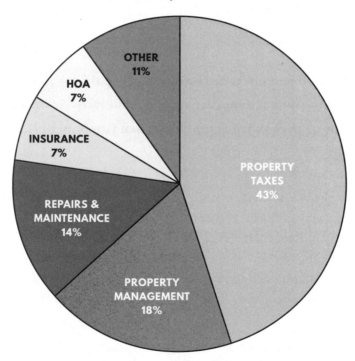

Green Street Advisors, "Single-Family Rental Primer," June 6, 2016

SAMPLE ANNUAL TAX SAVING CALCULATIONS

Annual Rent	**$20,000**
Annual Expenses (35%)	**($7,000)**
Net Operating Income	**$13,000**
Mortgage Interest	**($12,000)**
Net Income	**$1,000**
Depreciation Expense	**($8,500)**
(1/27.5 of building cost for residential rental real estate – buildings or structures and structural components)	
————————————————————	
Taxable Income (Loss)	**($7,500)**
Potential Savings	**$750 - $2,970**
(Assumes 10.0% – 39.6% tax bracket rates)	

This sample calculation shows a $7,500 loss which you would then enter into your IRS 1040 form to reduce your taxable income, therefore reducing your taxes. Potential annual savings depends on your income tax bracket.

What does that mean in the real world? As you can see in the example provided, when you add these expenses to your regular deductions for mortgage interest and depreciation, you can potentially show a loss that significantly reduces your overall taxable income.

In my experience, this fourth pillar is the most underrated of them all. Hey, whether it's rental income or a tax deduction, it's all money in the end, right? *Ka-ching!*

So there you have it: Rent Estate's four unique revenue generators. As you can see, the ultimate benefit of owning rental properties is that these elements work together to deliver financial freedom, retirement security, and—as people like J.D. Dickerson have already proven—happiness.

RENT ESTATE RECAP

A secure retirement has long been an essential part of the American Dream. But today, millions of people struggle to save enough money for retirement, and Social Security faces severe funding challenges. Rent Estate fills the gap, delivering four distinct points of value that make it an essential tool for achieving retirement security and financial freedom.

---

3 TAKEAWAYS

1. Most Americans are falling far short of being financially ready for retirement.

2. No matter how your personal retirement situation looks, adding a Rent Estate component can help you better diversify.

3. Only Rent Estate opens up four distinct revenue streams for you: long-term cash flow, equity, appreciation, and tax breaks.

ACTION ITEM

Check out the "*Ka-Ching!*" video at RentEstateRevolution.com.

CHAPTER 4

THE REVOLUTION IS FOR YOU

Scenario 1: A woman is so late on her mortgage payments that it threatens to ruin her credit rating.

Scenario 2: A recently engaged couple can't afford to sell their respective homes (or live in them), so they face the prospect of starting their marriage in bankruptcy.

Scenario 3: A family can't find good tenants for the rental home they inherited from their recently deceased father, and now it's costing them valuable time and money.

Housing sits at the center of our lives, and every big moment has implications for it: marriage, divorce, death, relocation, new jobs, retirement, you name it. But here's the thing: Each of the scenarios I've just outlined was solved by Rent Estate:

Scenario 1: The woman who was late on her mortgage payments was able to catch up (and save her credit rating) by renting her home.

Scenario 2: The recently engaged couple was able to afford a new home by renting both of their existing homes instead of trying to sell them.

Scenario 3: The family who inherited their dad's rental home hired a property management firm[1] to handle their tenant

---

1 Hint: I work for them.

placement. They saved time and money, but more importantly, they also kept their father's prized possession in the family.

By now, I hope you're convinced that the Rent Estate Revolution is real and here to stay. But that's just the first step. The next one is actually seeing yourself in it. And I suspect that your inner skeptic might have some thoughts on that.

THE SKEPTIC SPEAKS

"You make the case for different generations, but is Rent Estate really for regular people like me, or just those slick real estate mogul types? Isn't it too risky? Isn't it too late to take advantage of it? And don't you have a self-interest in promoting it?"

All good questions, so let's address them one at a time. Then we'll move on to the next two sections, where you can learn everything that's involved in Rent Estate, as well as the details of how to join the Revolution.

Is the Rent Estate Revolution really for people like me?

There's a reason I call Rent Estate "real estate for the rest of us." For too long, we've thought of real estate as some mysterious, private world for an elite class who already have a lot of money. We think of it like Wall Street. And when we're asked to picture a real estate mogul, our thoughts immediately go to tailored suits, slicked-back hair, and sketchy personalities.

Well, I'm not that guy. I'm the son of a cop. I had a regular job until I got laid off. And I don't have a Harvard MBA or any special training in real estate. I simply saw an opportunity, learned as I went along, and made the most of it. It's also worth noting that Renters Warehouse founder Brenton Hayden didn't even have a formal college education when he started the company; just a real estate license and a brilliant idea.

That's why when it comes to Rent Estate, I think of that scene in the movie *Rudy* where Rudy's father tries to convince him to abandon his dream of playing football for Notre Dame. "Notre Dame is for rich kids, smart kids, great athletes," the father says. "It's not for us!" I'm with Rudy when he later says, "My whole life, people have been telling me what I could do and I couldn't do. I've always listened to them. I don't want to do that anymore."

RENT ESTATE TURNS AROUND
MIDWESTERN NEIGHBORHOODS

For an example of how Rent Estate has the power to improve lives, communities, and entire cities, look no further than Rent Estate investor and Renters Warehouse client **Ed Renwick**.

Years ago, Ed set out to make urban housing more affordable—especially for single parents who are often priced out of the market or forced to live in shabby homes and apartments.

Ed looked at cities like St. Louis, Kansas City, and Cincinnati, and he saw a vicious circle. Landlords couldn't clear enough money, so they couldn't replace furnaces and make needed repairs. Rental homes fell into disrepair. And regular people couldn't get loans to buy them.

Ed has now snatched up over 1,700 Rent Estate properties in urban Midwestern neighborhoods. He buys them cheap, fixes them up, and rents them for affordable rates, generally $500–$850. Single parents and middle- to lower-middle-class families can afford the rent, and Ed can afford to keep up the homes—especially because he outsources his property management.

Ed's process creates a "virtuous circle" in which property values can rise as neighborhoods recover and thrive. And that's a real Rent Estate success story.

The truly amazing thing about Rent Estate is that if you already have a mortgage, you've already cleared the biggest hurdle in building your Rent Estate portfolio. If you own a home, you own a business, and that home is probably your biggest financial asset. So the logical question to ask is, "What's the best way to get the most money out of it?" To me, the answer is clear: Rent it out and then buy more rental properties.

As we'll see in Chapter 9, no financial instrument is more accessible to the average Joe or Jane than Rent Estate. I can't think of any other investment that lets you take greater advantage of financial leverage. In other words, Rent Estate is the only investment you can get a bank to finance, and then have someone else pay off. Think about it this way:

- A bank won't lend you money to buy stock in Apple, but it will lend you money to buy a property to rent.
- A random stranger would never agree to pay off your mortgage, but a tenant will.

That, in the smallest possible nutshell, is what makes Rent Estate unique (and forgive me if I repeat the point often). Tell me another investment that allows you to stand in the middle between a bank and a tenant and basically collect and cash the checks. It never ceases to amaze me.

Best of all—and I'm going to state this bluntly—no one gets screwed in Rent Estate. In fact, everyone wins. The bank makes a smart investment and gets paid back. The tenant pays what they can afford to live where they want. And you get to reap the benefits of setting up that system.

In fact, I would take it a step further: One of Rent Estate's virtues is that it does society a favor. Just as Uber and Airbnb argue that their models remove waste from the system by preventing cars and living spaces from sitting idle and unused, Rent Estate helps homeowners avoid eviction and foreclosure, helps tenants repair their credit,[2] and keeps homes livable and up to code.

In fact, by reducing the number of single-family homes that sit vacant, Rent Estate can help stabilize and raise property values, while also making homes less susceptible to crime. Most important, Rent Estate gives both landlords and tenants greater access to the American Dream of financial freedom and a secure retirement, which is what the Revolution is all about.

Is Rent Estate too risky as an investment opportunity?

We'll explore this even more in Chapter 9, but here's the top-level view: All investments carry risk; that's the nature of investing. But of all the opportunities you have, is there anything that provides a more consistent upside with a more minimal downside than Rent Estate? I don't think so, but don't take my word for it. Consider these facts:

- Home prices tend to be less volatile than stock market fluctuations.[3]

- Rental property cash flow is virtually recession-proof. Homes are like liquor stores: People need them in both good times and bad.

- Rent Estate is a better potential hedge against inflation than equities.[4] Rents can rise with inflation, but your mortgage payments don't.

- The value of your rental property also rises with inflation.

In short, it's hard to think of a time when Rent Estate doesn't work in your favor. People always need a place to live, no matter how good or bad the economy is. When home prices are high, fewer people can buy,

---

2   Renters Warehouse tenants can improve their credit because we report their on-time rent payments to Experian, one of the nation's top credit rating agencies.

3   Case Shiller home price index vs. the S&P 500 Index since 1987. Source: Diana Olick, "Where to Put Your Cash? A House or Stock," CNBC, December 8, 2014, www.cnbc.com/2014/12/08/where-to-put-your-cash-a-house-or-a-stock.html.

4   Kristin McFarland, "Why Real Estate Could Be a Better Investment Than Stocks," *U.S. News & World Report*, August 20, 2015, http://money.usnews.com/money/blogs/the-smarter-mutual-fund-investor/2015/08/20/why-real-estate-could-be-a-better-investment-than-stocks.

more need to rent, and you can charge more. When home prices dip, you can snatch up more rental properties and still find great tenants.

In a way, this is similar to the benefit of buying stocks: When they're up, you're making money; when they're down, you can buy more at bargain prices. The difference is that Rent Estate is structured to deliver more stability than the stock market. Plus, you have no real control of a stock's value. With a rental property, you can always *add* value.

A further stabilizing force in Rent Estate occurred during the development of *Rent Estate Revolution*: Fannie Mae, the mortgage guarantor controlled by the federal government, announced that it was starting to back debt related to single-family rental homes.[5] In plain language, that means that the government recognizes the fact that homeownership is being replaced by "homerentership," and is actively *fueling* the movement.

Fannie Mae's move should make it easier for investors to buy and hold single-family properties, leading to more homes turning into rentals, more supply for future Rent Estate investors like you to choose from, and potentially even less risk in the Rent Estate market as a whole. And that's good news.

Is it already too late to take advantage of Rent Estate?

This is a great question, because with so many investments, by the time you finally catch wind of them, it's way too late to make any money.

In the early days of the Internet, raking in a fortune was relatively easy—just ask the founders of Netscape and Cisco Systems. But it's always the *insiders* who get in first on any disruptive phenomenon. As the concept matures and spreads to the masses, regular folks are often left out in the cold. (Case in point: By the time a business guru goes on television to insist that you buy a certain stock, chances are his "hot tip" has already gone cold.)

---

5   Teke Wiggin, "Fannie Mae Takes Steps That May Fuel Single-Family Rental Growth," Inman, February 2017, www.inman.com/2017/01/27/fannie-mae-takes-step-that-may-fuel-single-family-rental-growth/amp/.

Rent Estate is different. As I've said previously, we're only at the beginning of the Rent Estate Revolution. Or to go back to my forest analogy, the fires of the Great Recession have burned down the old forest of traditional real estate. But the new forest of Rent Estate is still in the sapling phase.

This isn't a gut feeling; it's based on hard-core statistics. As I pointed out in Chapter 2, U.S. homeownership is expected to decline for at least the next 15 years, new renters are expected to outnumber new homeowners for the first time ever, and most families who have lost their homes are unlikely to become homeowners again.[6]

Now let's add on the well-documented "life delay" trend among younger generations. People are increasingly putting off marriage and kids, which are the traditional catalysts for settling down and buying a home. In 1990, the average man and woman got married at 26 and 23, respectively. Now those averages have risen to 29 and 27.[7] Parenthood shows the same momentum. In the last 45 years, the average age of a first-time mom has increased from 21.4 years old to 26.3.[8]

RENT ESTATE REMINDER
The Rent Estate market is definitely established, but it also has lots of room for growth as more and more families turn to renting single-family homes vs. buying.

6　Laura Kusisto, "Many Who Lost Homes to Foreclosure in Last Decade Won't Return—NAR," *The Wall Street Journal,* April 20, 2015, https://www.wsj.com/articles/many-who-lost-homes-to-foreclosure-in-last-decade-wont-return-nar-1429548640.

7　Kelsey Borreson, "5 Good Reasons to Get Married While You're Young, According to Research," The Huffington Post, updated November 14, 2013, www.huffingtonpost.com/2013/11/14/married-young_n_4227924.html.

8　Rae Ellen Bichell, "Average Age of First-Time Moms Keeps Climbing in the U.S.," National Public Radio, January 14, 2016, http://www.npr.org/sections/health-shots/2016/01/14/462816458/average-age-of-first-time-moms-keeps-climbing-in-the-u-s.

Again, there's no sign of these trends reversing. And while they touch on a wide variety of social, financial, and demographic realities, they all add up to one thing: a strong demand for rentals. Bottom line: Single-family housing makes up nearly 40 percent of the overall rental stock[9] and provides homes for 22.4 million households[10]. That sounds like a big number until you realize that there are nearly 117 million total households in the U.S.[11] I'd call that "room for growth."

Do you have a self-interest in spurring this movement?

I'm the CEO of the nation's largest property management firm for single-family rentals. So on one hand, I absolutely have a self-interest in inspiring more people to join the Rent Estate Revolution. The more people who buy rental properties, the greater need they'll have for affordable and airtight property management. So I guess you got me.

Except for this: By drawing more attention to this movement, I'm also encouraging more entrepreneurs to enter the market and compete with Renters Warehouse. Why would I want that? Because I believe in capitalism and the free market. Competition makes this country run, and I'm confident that my company has the drive and talent to stay ahead.

More important, I've seen too many people left out of the American Dream. I've seen too many couples arrive at their senior years in a state of financial insecurity. And I think Rent Estate is the key to bringing retirement security back to this country.

In short, I believe both in the mantra of personal responsibility *and* the idea that a rising tide lifts all boats. We all have a stake in each

---

9   Joint Center for Housing Studies of Harvard University, "The State of the Nation's Housing, 2015," June 24, 2015, http://www.jchs.harvard.edu/sites/jchs.harvard.edu/files/jchs-sonhr-2015-ch1.pdf.

10 Tribune Wire Reports, "More Than Half of U.S. Renters Older Than 40, Study Says," *Chicago Tribune*, December 9, 2015, http://www.chicagotribune.com/business/ct-renters-older-than-40-20151209-story.html.

11 U.S. Census Bureau, "Households and Families: 2010," April 2012, https://www.census.gov/prod/cen2010/briefs/c2010br-14.pdf.

other's success. So in that sense, yes, I do have a self-interest in writing this book (and I make no apologies for that). I also hope you see your own self-interest in reading it.

RENT ESTATE RECAP

You should join the Rent Estate Revolution because it's amazingly accessible for regular folks, it's impressively high-reward/low-risk relative to other investments, and we're still in the early stages of a movement with plenty of upside.

---

3 TAKEAWAYS

1. The Rent Estate Revolution is available to everyone, not just a select few.

2. If you already have a mortgage, you're already well on your way to becoming a Rent Estate Entrepreneur.

3. Rent Estate is generally less volatile, more reliable, and more recession-proof than equities and other traditional investment tools.

ACTION ITEM

Download "The Insider's Guide to Rent Estate" at RentEstateRevolution.com.

SECTION 1

SUMMARY

The real estate landscape has changed permanently, and the sooner you accept that we live in a new world, the better off you'll be. Today, Rent Estate is the new real estate. It's more accessible, easier to manage, less risky, and potentially more lucrative than traditional real estate ever was. It's "real estate for the rest of us."

In a nutshell, Rent Estate is about opening the doors to financial freedom and a secure retirement by purchasing and renting out single-family homes. It isn't about buying commercial real estate, apartments, or condos. It's "buy and hold," not "buy and flip."

For skeptics who might dismiss Rent Estate as a trend or fad, consider the data. Homeownership in America has fallen to its lowest level since 1965 and is expected to decline at least until 2030. Less than a third of families who lost their homes in the past decade are likely to become homeowners again. And all generations—Baby Boomers, Gen Xers, and Millennials alike—are embracing renting like never before.

In an age of volatility and weakening Social Security, Rent Estate opens the doors to retirement security and financial freedom in four ways that traditional real estate can't: long-term cash flow, equity, appreciation, and tax breaks. This makes Rent Estate incredibly reliable and recession-proof compared with other investments.

Finally, it's still early to join the Rent Estate Revolution. The number of single-family homes being used as rentals is growing rapidly, but it's still a small share of the overall market. If you already have a mortgage, you're well on your way. The next step is understanding more about exactly what Rent Estate entails—especially the ins and outs of property management—so you can strategize on what to do yourself vs. having others do it for you.

SECTION II
THE RENT ESTATE
LANDSCAPE

If you're still reading this book, then you're at least intrigued by the possibilities that Rent Estate presents. Good. That means you don't think I'm crazy when I say that a perfect storm has permanently changed the real estate landscape to your potential benefit.

But now that we've looked at the 30,000-foot view, let's begin our descent. In other words, let's get under the clouds and start clarifying some Rent Estate details. As you're about to see, it's a big and complex landscape.

If you can successfully navigate these areas, then you can reap the substantial rewards of the Rent Estate Revolution. And the especially good news is this: Managing a Rent Estate Empire has never been easier or more accessible than it is right now.

So make sure your seat back is in its upright and locked position, and let's look outside the window at your future in Rent Estate.

CHAPTER 5

THE TENETS OF TENANTS

When I moved from Phoenix to Minneapolis, I rented my Arizona home to a guy we'll call Ron. Ron was there for seven years, so I got to know him pretty well. And it came as a shock when he sent me a text one day telling me that his wife had left him and he couldn't afford the rent. He was looking for a roommate to help out, but in the meantime, could I be flexible?

As we'll see, the answer to this question should usually be "no." But I knew Ron well enough to take a chance on him. I worked with him, and thankfully, the story has a happy ending. Not only did Ron eventually get back up to date on his payments, but one day I got a note in the mail that read: "Thanks for your help. Julie and I got back together! —Ron."

I mention this story because when we talk about real estate, it's easy to focus on "things": land, property, numbers, graphs, projections. It can sound cold and calculating, and to a large extent, it is. But Rent Estate is different, because it's fundamentally about *people*.

Don't get me wrong: Numbers matter in Rent Estate. But Rent Estate is a human business at its core. You're trying to improve your life by working toward financial freedom. But unlike buy-and-flip real estate, you depend on tenants. And they're not just numbers on a page. They're real people living real lives.

It's not a requirement that you get to know the individuals and families who inhabit your property, but it does enhance the experience. I can tell you firsthand: People are one of the most rewarding aspects of Rent Estate. Our Renters Warehouse clients talk all the time about how they consider their renters like family, and that bond makes them feel even better about what they're doing.

Unfortunately, the term "tenant" doesn't quite capture the nature of the relationship in Rent Estate. I've always thought it sounded a bit medieval, and it actually is.[1]

Thankfully, we live in a different age now. But it's hard to shake the old-fashioned image of wealthy landowners "lording" over the people living on their property.

That being said, *tenant* is the proper legal term for a renter. So I'll use both terms. But I urge you to think of the people living in your properties as that: *people*. Like you, they're also looking for a better life—a great home in a great neighborhood, and a place to start and raise a family.

It's also important to think of your tenants as your business partners. Anyone experienced in Rent Estate will tell you that the difference between a bad tenant and a good tenant is not only the difference between cash congestion and cash flow; it's also the difference between misery and happiness.

Good property managers don't look for just good tenants; they shoot for *great* tenants. Great tenants respect your property, always pay the rent in full and on time, and help you open those doors to financial freedom.

---

1 For over a thousand years, medieval European landlords literally owned their tenants. *Tenant* comes from the Anglo-French *tenir*, which means "to hold," as in "to own."

THE SKEPTIC SPEAKS

"That's all well and good, but I assume that great tenants don't grow on trees. Are they really out there, and if so, how do you find them?"

Glad you asked. Let's dig in.

Crunching the Magic Number

First, we need to talk about numbers. Perhaps the most important consideration in attracting great tenants is determining what you're going to ask them to pay in rent. Finding the magic rent number isn't as easy as you might think, and there's a lot at stake. Set it too low, and a long lease agreement might handcuff your ability to achieve positive cash flow for several years. Set it too high, and your house might sit vacant on the market, earning nothing.

You need to determine the sweet spot that's low enough to attract people, yet high enough to deliver maximum value to you. So many factors go into finding that number, you practically need a Google algorithm to find it. What's the square footage? How many bedrooms and bathrooms are there? Is the house furnished or unfurnished? How modern are the amenities? Is it close to good schools, parks, a nice grocery store, or a Starbucks? How's the landscaping? Does it have a two-car garage? Can you sleep well at night, or do police sirens blare at 2 A.M.? And most important, is there a ferret infestation?

(Okay, I made that last one up. Just seeing if you're paying attention.) The point is, determining the right rent number is complicated. And frankly, it's better to tap third-party resources instead of trying to find it yourself.

FIND OUT HOW MUCH YOUR HOME WILL RENT FOR @ RentEstateRevolution.com

But once you have a great property and know the magic rent number, then what? How do you start marketing the property to pull in potential renters?

Attracting the Right Leads

The way to advertise homes for rent has changed ridiculously fast in the last decade. Not too long ago, most of the marketing power was in the property owner's hands. All you had to do was hold up a giant tenant magnet in the form of an ad in your local newspaper, or a post on Craigslist, and then sit back and wait for the phone to ring or the emails to come in.

As with everything else, the Internet changed all that. Today, the digital marketplace is expansive, competitive, and highly fragmented. Combine that with a hot overall rental market, and *voilà!* The customer has more power than ever before.

If you're truly looking for great tenants, then it's a renter's market. They're the magnets, not you. Without leaving their desks, today's renters can cast their nets wider than ever before. They can instantly research multiple properties across specialized databases. They can comparison shop with a single mouse click. And don't forget this: They can unearth your reputation as a landlord and make or break that reputation by writing reviews for the entire world to see.

I didn't invent the term *trust economy*, but I agree that we're living in it. With the ability to instantly review anyone and anything, trust and good customer service are more important now than ever. In fact, the landlord-tenant relationship is increasingly like the Uber driver-passenger dynamic: I review you; you review me. On a level playing field of mutually assured success or destruction, everyone needs to be on their best behavior.

IF YOU WANT TO TRY ADVERTISING YOUR PROPERTY ON YOUR OWN, DOWNLOAD OUR GUIDE "HOW TO CREATE A SUCCESSFUL RENTAL AD" @ RentEstateRevolution.com

Tapping the Right Media

As a property owner, you need to reach empowered consumers in the most efficient and cost-effective way possible, which is definitely *not* running a 1/8-page ad in the dead-tree edition of the local news. Today's complete to-do list for marketing a rental property looks like this:

RENTAL PROPERTY MARKETING TO-DO LIST (PARTIAL)

☐ Thoroughly clean and stage the property inside and out.

☐ Take professional photographs of every room. Create a virtual tour of the entire property.

☐ Create a unique website for the property. Research hundreds of rental property websites.

☐ Create unique ads for each website (and pay for them).

☐ Don't forget those free online resources like Craigslist.

☐ Create flyers for bulletin boards in local coffee shops. Design ads for free rental publications and magazines.

☐ Develop relationships with local real estate agents. Create yard signs.

☐ Continually monitor all online activity on every website.

☐ Tweak ad copy, photos, and videos as needed.

Does this list make your head spin? It should, but it reflects the media world we now live in. Great tenants are out there, but *they're in control.* They have the resources at their fingertips to find the perfect home. It's your responsibility to rise to the top of their list.

Before you stress out too much, here's the good news: You don't have to go it alone when it comes to tenant marketing. One of the reasons property management firms exist is because they've found a way to make finding tenants more organized, effective, efficient, manageable, and affordable. As we'll see, tenant marketing is just one of many areas where third-party providers are relieving Rent Estate Entrepreneurs of their day-to-day headaches.

Converting Good Leads into Great Tenants

Let's say you did everything in that long to-do list. You got some good nibbles, so you're close to finding a great tenant, right? Maybe. But you'll need to go through four additional processes to fully seal the deal: application, verification and screening, leases, and inspections. All of these are important, so let's touch on each.

Application

The first thing you'll need to do is create a Rental Application Form and a Tenant Reference Form. These documents are designed to give you key personal, employment, and other information—including the tenant's date of birth, Social Security number, current address, employer name, job description, length of employment, length of time at current address, and current landlord's name and contact information, to name a few.

These forms are also useful in gleaning other important information. *How many people and pets will be living on the property?*

TENANT INFORMATION SECURITY TIPS

☐ Don't release tenant financial or personal data to a third party (e.g., debt collectors) without the tenant's written consent.

☐ When not in use, always keep paper-based tenant records under lock and key.

☐ Password-protect all confidential tenant files that are in digital format.

☐ Shred nonessential tenant files.

Has the tenant has ever filed for bankruptcy? Have they ever faced eviction or been arrested?

It should go without saying, but I'll say it anyway: You need to guard all this information with your life. These people are entrusting you with personal data that could lead to identity theft or other issues if placed in the wrong hands.

DOWNLOAD SAMPLE RENTAL APPLICATION AND TENANT REFERENCE FORMS @
RentEstateRevolution.com

Verification and Screening
So you've supplied the forms, and your potential tenant has filled them out. Now the fun part begins: verifying that information and digging a little deeper—maybe a lot deeper. This amounts to conducting four different kinds of checks: rental history, credit history, background information, and references. As part of this, you might do some or all of the following.

- Mine various online databases to find the renter's rental history, including evictions.[2]

- Call former landlords to find out what kind of tenant the applicant was.

- Tap resources like Equifax, TransUnion, and Experian to run credit reports.

- Call the person's employer to verify their hire date, employment status, and income.

- Request tax returns to verify income, especially if the tenant is self-employed.

2 Examples: www.myrentalhistoryreport.com, www.experian.com/rentbureau/rental-history.html, www.myrental.com, www.tenantbackgroundsearch.com

---

TENANT SCREENING TIPS

☐ Don't just look at a potential tenant's current landlord; look at their last *two*.

☐ Check the address that a potential tenant gives you for their current residence (it might be their Uncle Dave).

☐ Contact their employer. People have been known to invent companies and forge pay stubs.

- Run a criminal history report.

- Contact the tenant's personal references. Yes, a renter would be crazy to give you the name of someone who doesn't like them. But it's always a good idea to verify that someone's personal references actually exist.

- Check out the tenant's social media presence. Make sure these are public accounts and that you do it for every tenant, not just some. And be careful. You can't refuse a tenant if you don't like their political beliefs, but you can if their social media accounts indicate that they lied about having a pet.

Keep in mind that the Fair Housing Act applies to most single-family rentals. As a landlord, you can reject a tenant based on some criteria, but definitely not others.

Leases

Tenant leases are legally binding agreements that specify everything from move-in dates and security deposits to when the rent is due and how to report a maintenance issue. But here's the most important thing to remember about them:

Lease agreements are your number-one conflict-avoidance and litigation-prevention tools.

You can start by grabbing a template off of the web, but make the extra effort to customize it to produce the most legally airtight lease agreement possible. Since landlord/tenant laws vary from state to state, your leases need to be state-specific. But they should also be tenant-specific to prevent accusations of favoritism or discrimination. Here's a sample of the clauses and provisions you should include in any lease agreement:

- **Full Names of All Tenant Occupants**. This makes each adult tenant legally responsible for the terms of the lease. It also allows you to seek rent from any of the occupants, while also enabling you to terminate the lease should even one of the occupants violate any of its terms.

- **Rent Specs**. Include the amount of rent being paid, to whom and when, as well as the payment terms and which forms of payment will be accepted. Also be sure to include as much information as you can about late fees, including if they can be incurred and how high they can be.

You can screen prospective tenants based on these factors . . .	. . . but not these.
✓ Credit history	✗ Race or color
✓ Income	✗ National origin
✓ History of not paying rent	✗ Religion
✓ Prior bankruptcies	✗ Disability or handicap, including physical or mental impairment
✓ References	
✓ Some types of criminal convictions	✗ Sex
	✗ Familial status (includes protection for people with children under age 18 or pregnant women)

- **Security Deposit Specs**. Security deposits are a common source of dispute between landlords and tenants. To prevent hassles and legal issues, be sure to include the amount of the deposit, how you may use it, and when and how you'll return it. And make sure you're compliant with state and local laws.[3]

- **Maintenance, Utilities, and Extras**. List who's responsible for paying which expenses, as well as which party is responsible for performing various maintenance tasks, such as mowing lawns and changing lightbulbs.

- **Pets**. Specify whether pets are allowed in the rental, which kinds (are you "ferret friendly"?), and all relevant conditions. Let renters know if you charge a pet fee or require a pet deposit.

DOWNLOAD "SIT! STAY! WHAT YOU SHOULD KNOW ABOUT RENTING TO PET OWNERS" @ RentEstateRevolution.com

- **Destruction of Property**. Regular wear and tear is expected, so you need to spell out the difference between "wear and tear" and "destruction of property." (We delve deeper into this topic in Chapter 7, "The Art of Conflict.")

- **Alterations to Property**. If a tenant wants to make physical changes to your property, it's best to clarify the parameters and permissions up front in as much detail as possible.

- **Change of Terms**. If you'd like to make changes to the terms of a lease without ending it, you can. Specify in the lease that written mutual consent by both landlord and tenant allows you to amend the terms of the lease.

- **Right to Entry and Inspection**. You'll need access to the rental for maintenance, emergencies, and re-renting the property.

---

3 Nolo.com provides an excellent resource for researching the various state laws related to security deposits: www.nolo.com/legal-encyclopedia/security-deposit-limits-deadlines-your-state-36186.html.

Detail the conditions under which you are allowed to enter the premises, and how much notice you need to give.

- **Criminal Activity**. Detail the types of activity that you will not tolerate on your property. A Crime Free Lease Addendum might be required in your city or state. This is a civil contract between you and your tenant in which the rental applicant agrees to abide by the rules of the property, and not to participate in or allow criminal activity to occur in and around your property.

VIEW SAMPLE CRIME FREE LEASE ADDENDUM LANGUAGE @ RentEstateRevolution.com

- **Insurance**. You'll need to look into a landlord and rental dwelling policy, which is different from a standard homeowners policy. These policies provide coverage for physical damage caused by the usual "acts of God," as well as personal property you might leave on-site for maintenance or tenant use (e.g., appliances) and liability coverage if a tenant gets hurt on your property. They don't, however, cover your *tenants'* personal possessions. So to avoid disputes, consider requiring tenants to buy their own renters insurance.

- **Partial Invalidity**. If part of the rental agreement is deemed invalid, then this clause can help ensure that the remainder of the agreement still applies.

- **No Waiver**. If you choose not to strictly enforce the contract terms (e.g., the rent is paid late but you let the late fee slide), this clause provides that you don't waive your right to enforce lease compliance in the future.

Even if you feel good about your leases, you should always have an attorney look at them to dot the i's and cross the t's on relevant federal, state, and local laws. Better yet, hire a professional property management company to handle them for you. It's one more thing to take off your plate so you can take full advantage of Rent Estate.

Inspections

After the lease is signed, it's time for the move-in inspection. The main issue here is the security deposit. When you and your tenants are on the same page from the beginning, there's a much lower chance that you'll disagree on what, if anything, should be deducted from that deposit when they leave.

A proper move-in inspection involves you and your tenants walking through the entire property as you fill out an inspection form (or having a property management company do this for you—especially if you don't live close to the property). Carefully note the condition of each room, preferably documenting everything using photos and/or video. Then have all parties sign the form. This way, you have everyone agreeing on the home's condition from day one.

The move-out inspection simply repeats this process, providing an objective basis for deciding how much of the tenant's deposit should be refunded. Between move-in and move-out, you should also conduct random and routine inspections throughout the tenant life cycle.

> **"As property management firms grow more professional and offer more services, it doesn't always make sense to DIY tenant placement."**

Having tenants involves a fair amount of work in different areas before they move in. With that in mind, I now introduce a feature you'll see throughout Section II: **DIY Downsides/Outsourcing Upsides**. I include it because I'm the poster child for the perils and pitfalls of going DIY (do-it-yourself). I tried it during my time in Arizona, and I learned how hard it is to maintain—especially as you take on more and more properties. As property management firms grow more professional and offer more services, it doesn't always make sense to DIY tenant placement.

DIY Downsides/Outsourcing Upsides: Finding Great Tenants

DIY Downsides

- **"Renters Roulette."** When you go it alone, you run the risk of wasting multiple afternoons flipping through renter applications—not to mention running credit, rental, and criminal background checks on every potential tenant. Maybe you're into that kind of thing, but I'd rather go golfing.

- **Marketing Hassle.** Are you the most qualified person to handle photography, virtual tour production, web development, and search engine marketing for your properties? Usually, these disciplines are best left to professionals—especially when it comes to marketing copy. I know everyone thinks they're a writer (including me), but not everyone writes good.[4]

- **Getting Sued.** Once you secure a tenant, the red tape can get pretty thick. Now you have to deal with lease documents and inspections, and there's no margin for error. Some provisions in boilerplate lease contracts may not apply to your state. Some might actually be illegal. Do you want to run that risk?

Outsourcing Upsides

- **Greater Speed.** Property management technologies exist to create a website for your property and market it quickly to millions of potential renters. They hit the rental websites and find the qualified candidates. You decide who rents. (For example, Renters Warehouse uses technology to score tenants in 11–17 days on average.)

- **Easier Background Checks.** All that verification work? Forget about it. You should be able to outsource background

---

4   See what I did there?

and credit checks on each potential tenant. The result is usually a higher-quality tenant than you could find on your own, faster.

- **Tenant Turnover.** In my experience, the cost of losing a tenant can equal two to three months' rent—and that's not including actual lost rent. Some property management companies offer what's essentially a tenant warranty. For six months or longer, they'll warranty the tenants they find for your property. If those tenants default for any reason, they'll provide additional tenant placement services at no cost to you.[5]

---

5   I have to admit, Renters Warehouse is actually the only property management company I know of that offers this service. Our tenant warranty programs can run from 6 to 18 months.

RENT ESTATE RECAP

Great tenants are the engine that makes Rent Estate run. From knowing what to charge in rent to writing legally airtight lease agreements, every decision you make potentially impacts your ability to achieve financial freedom. That's why you should consider outsourcing tenant placement rather than trying to do it all on your own.

3 TAKEAWAYS

1. Rent Estate is a people business. But to make it work, you need great tenants who respect your property, do their part to maintain it, and pay the rent on time, every time.

2. Today, finding great tenants is a lot more complicated than running an ad in the local newspaper or posting on Craigslist. You need to reach the right people, when and how they want to be reached, in many different mediums.

3. Luckily, it's never been easier or more affordable to turn the complexities of tenant placement over to experienced professionals.

ACTION ITEM

Download the "How to Perfect the Tenant Placement Process" guide at RentEstateRevolution.com.

CHAPTER 6

RENT COLLECTION AND THE DAILY GRIND

I used to pester my Gen X neighbor (call him "Nick") over beers at our annual block parties. Nick knew that I ran a property management firm, and I knew that he ran himself ragged trying to manage five rental properties. In addition to having a full-time job, Nick was a classic DIYer. He wanted to buy more properties, but he could never find the time.

I made it my mission to get Nick to outsource his property management, and eventually, I wore him down. He outsourced his headaches, and with the extra time and money, he bought three additional properties, and is eyeing more. The added cash flow is primed to help with college payments for his kids. And for him and his wife, the equity and appreciation are now a big part of their retirement portfolio.

I know lots of cases like Nick's, and what they illustrate is the fact that in Rent Estate, securing great tenants is just the beginning. Once you have people actually living in your property, you can run into a series of nonstop headaches if you don't manage things right. Remember: Rent Estate is about freedom, so fixing an air conditioner at 3 A.M. doesn't exactly meet that threshold.

The People Factor

You know all my talk about how Rent Estate is a people-oriented business? How you need to see your tenants almost like family—and how we live in a trust-based society where complete strangers can make or break your reputation? Well, this is where the rubber meets the road.

Remember: You're running a business here. Your properties are your shops, and your tenants are your customers. It's not enough that you got them through the door and into your house. You need to keep them happy and loyal so they'll recommend you to their friends and say good things about you online.

So if there's one overarching piece of advice I can give you about property management, it's this:

Be proactive, not reactive.

In other words, don't hope for the best and wait to deal with stuff as it comes up. Have a plan. Take preventive measures. Form a rapid-response dream team of maintenance superheroes to deal with issues that arise. Make sure that repetitive tasks happen like clockwork, and that miscellaneous issues are dealt with quickly and completely. The Golden Rule applies as much to property management as anything else: Treat your tenants as you would want to be treated.

Now let's talk about the daily grind so you can see how much of it you're comfortable handling on your own vs. having a professional property manager do it for you.

The Rent Revolution

Collecting the rent makes up both the "cash" and the "flow" in "cash flow." But rent collection should be an out-of-sight, out-of-mind process for both you and your tenants. If your leases are precise, it will be. Because you'll clearly specify not only the amount of rent and when it's due, but also the penalties your tenants will incur if they're late in paying.

That last part is more important than you might think. Not charging penalties works against your financial interests. It also sets a bad precedent that can become a legal issue, as creating an atmosphere of mutual disregard for one part of a lease makes it harder to enforce other parts that may cause conflict down the line.

Keep in mind that the identity profiles of renters have changed drastically over the last decade. As we've already touched on, young adults used to be the most popular renting demographic. But now Gen Xers and Baby Boomers make up a growing part of the picture. In fact—and this may surprise you, because it still surprises me—a majority of renters are now over the age of 40.[1]

This means two things when it comes to rent collection. First, your tenants will run the gamut on technological expertise and concerns about data privacy (don't be surprised if one tenant wants to submit the rent using Apple Pay and another would prefer to write a check and send it snail mail). Second, and perhaps more important, older adults generally have higher incomes and pay a smaller share of it on housing. The good news for you: You might have more leeway to raise the rent when necessary.

DOWNLOAD AN OVERVIEW
"RENT COLLECTION CHART"
@ RentEstateRevolution.com

Knowing the Law

As the landlord, you're responsible for being intimately familiar with landlord/tenant law. These laws vary considerably from state to state, and it's important to keep up on federal, state, and municipal levels. For example, most states have clear stipulations on how quickly you're required to respond to issues, as well as guidelines on keeping your properties structurally safe and habitable.

---

1 Tribune Wire Reports, "More Than Half of U.S. Renters Older Than 40, Study Says," *Chicago Tribune*, December 9, 2015, http://www.chicagotribune.com/business/ct-renters-older-than-40-20151209-story.html.

In general, you're always responsible for the basics. That means *you* should discover issues in these areas long before your tenants do:

- Clean running water
- Electricity
- Heating
- Adequate weatherproofing
- Sanitary conditions

If a tenant makes a maintenance request regarding these or any other issues, you need to create an action plan for repairs as soon as possible.

Maintenance Requests

Once you enter the world of Rent Estate, nothing is more unpredictable, inevitable, and potentially time-consuming than fielding maintenance requests from your tenants. Depending on how many properties you own, you can expect issues ranging from broken dishwashers and air conditioners to clogged toilets and ant infestations. And ask any rental property owner: These requests have an uncanny ability to rise when you're deep in REM sleep or on vacation.

RENT ESTATE REMINDER
You never know when the water heater or refrigerator will go out, so always budget for unexpected repairs and maintenance issues. As a general rule, set aside 1–2% of your property's value for annual maintenance.

But remember: No matter how trivial a maintenance request might sound, you need to take it seriously. Consider this cautionary tale from real estate investor and popular blogger Kevin Perk. He once received a phone call from a tenant saying that his phone charger had

```
┌─────────────────────────────────────────────────────────┐
│                 YOUR MAINTENANCE TEAM                    │
│                                                          │
│   ☐ Carpet Installer   ☐ Handyperson      ☐ Locksmith   │
│                                                          │
│   ☐ Cleaner            ☐ Heating/         ☐ Painter     │
│                           Cooling Expert                 │
│   ☐ Contractor                            ☐ Plumber     │
│                        ☐ Landscaper                      │
│   ☐ Electrician                           ☐ Snow Removal │
│                        ☐ Lawn Care                       │
│   ☐ Exterminator                                         │
│                                                          │
└─────────────────────────────────────────────────────────┘
```

melted while being plugged into a home outlet. When Kevin arrived at the property, he noticed that one of the electric meter's ceramic connections had cracked. Power was surging throughout the system. Fortunately, he was able to shut off the power before the entire property went up in flames[2].

Even though most of your day-to-day tenant requests won't be this dramatic, they'll still require dozens of important decisions on your part. Farming out these requests is the biggest no-brainer in Rent Estate. But before we get to that, let's take a look at some of the things you'll need to do to maintain your rental properties and keep your tenants happy.

Assembling Your Dream Team

Your rapid-response team of maintenance superstars is your biggest ally. So you need to partner with people who share your values in terms of quality, cost-effectiveness, and customer service. Once you find them, keep their contact information within easy reach. If an emergency comes up, you can't afford to waste time scrambling to find a phone number.

I can tell you from personal experience: Whether you or your property managers work directly with these people, they're some of your most important partners.

---

2   Kevin Perk, "When Is a Landlord's Maintenance Emergency Truly an Emergency?" Bigger Pockets, December 10, 2012, https://www.biggerpockets.com/renewsblog/2012/12/10/landlord-maintenance-emergency/.

Emergencies vs. Non-Emergencies

Maintenance requests come in three basic categories: 1) minor issues, like kitchen cabinets that don't shut right; 2) moderate issues, like clogged sinks or malfunctioning dishwashers; and 3) emergencies.

For the first two categories, your tenants should be able to reach you easily via phone, email, or text. And you should address them in a reasonable time frame—within a week for minor issues, and 48 hours for more serious issues like malfunctioning appliances.

Emergencies are a different story. You should always provide your tenants with a special number for anything related to water, heating, electricity, leaky roofs, serious plumbing problems, and, of course, anything involving "melting," "burning," or "smelling like gas." These issues require the modern equivalent of a Bat Phone, and they need to be addressed and repaired immediately.

Starting with the lease itself, make sure your tenants are clear about what constitutes an emergency, and what number to call or text when issues do crop up.

To DIY or Not to DIY

Some people can do virtually anything related to home repair; others are comfortable installing a dryer, but won't touch electrical work. Even those who hire out maintenance and repair work will often supervise their contractors, because they need to feel like they're in control of the process.

No matter how many properties you rent out, an overall maintenance strategy is critical. If you hire out the work yourself, you'll need to get competitive bids on each significant project. And that means contacting multiple contractors and providing each with a high level of detail. (It's not unheard of for this process to take longer than the work itself.) Once the work is done, you'll need your repair vendors to provide before-and-after photos or videos, as well as invoices and warranty information for your records. No matter who does the work, you must let your tenants know how long it'll take and when people will be entering the house. Once the work is done, always get the tenant's signature verifying that the project was completed to their satisfaction. This helps avert subsequent disputes, as some people could allege later (especially when they move out) that a repair wasn't properly addressed.

Better yet, consider outsourcing the entire headache to someone else—so you don't have to do the grunt work or the paperwork.

THE SKEPTIC SPEAKS

"I'm as good as any handyman, electrician, plumber, or carpenter I know, so why wouldn't I handle these tasks myself and save the time, money, and hassle of dealing with outside contractors?"

Many Renters Warehouse clients spend years trying to handle maintenance and repair work themselves—only to realize that by trying to control everything related to their rental properties, they lose control of what matters most: their family life. The benefit of working with a property management firm is that it frees you from all of this, and usually saves you money in the process.

DIY Downsides/Outsourcing Upsides: Rent Collection and the Daily Grind

DIY Downsides

- **Time Commitments.** Depending on the number of properties you're trying to manage, collecting rent and trafficking maintenance and repair requests can be a full-time job. If you prefer to handle most maintenance work yourself, be prepared to put a lot of your social and family life on hold.

- **The Vetting Headache.** If you're not already familiar with the contractors, electricians, and plumbers in the areas where you own property, figuring out who to trust can be a trial-and-error process. And you can't afford too many errors.

- **Leaky Toilet Syndrome.** At Renters Warehouse, this is what we call the affliction of always expecting the phone to ring at 2 A.M. with another gross plumbing issue. Fact is, if you're a DIYer, you always have to be within an arm's length of your phone. And that's never a good thing.

Outsourcing Upsides

- **Rent Payments in Your Account, Like Magic.** A good property manager will work to collect your rent for you—in full, on time, every month. They should be able to handle virtually any form of payment, including electronic funds transfer (EFT). And they should send free direct deposits to your bank account while providing monthly statements for your records.

- **No Bat Phone Needed.** Your property management company should be on call and on the case 24/7. Whether it's routine maintenance or a pressing emergency, that first phone call should always go to them, not you. So keep sleeping.

- **Vetting and Competitive Bids, Off Your Plate.** A good property management company should know your local market and have strong existing relationships with contractors for everything from lawn care to bathroom tiling. You work with them, they work with the contractors.

RENT ESTATE RECAP

Once you've secured great tenants, then the fun really begins. Some people enjoy the daily grind of collecting rent, doing inspections, and trafficking maintenance calls. But the true power of Rent Estate lies in your ability to hire a professional property management company to handle these and other tasks for you. A good property manager saves you time, money, and headaches, which delivers peace of mind and frees you to do the things you really love to do. Like buy more rental properties.

---

3 TAKEAWAYS

1. Once you have renters, you need to keep them happy by making rent collection and maintenance as easy as possible. Happier tenants means more lease renewals and a better reputation for you, which makes it even easier to find future tenants.

2. Being a DIY landlord can cost significant time and money. The more you try to handle everything yourself, the more likely you'll get sucked into an endless cycle of reaction, problem-solving, and legal disputes.

3. A professional property manager will handle tasks like rent collection, inspections, repair requests, and contractor bids—giving you the most important asset of all: freedom.

ACTION ITEM

Download "The Complete Guide to Rent Estate Landlording" at RentEstateRevolution.com.

CHAPTER 7

THE ART OF CONFLICT

My brother, Jon, is often my partner in personal Rent Estate deals, and he's always been remarkably fearless when It comes to tenant conflicts. Case in point. After spending days calling and emailing a Minneapolis tenant who was late with the rent, he decided to pay a visit to the home. Jon got no response when he knocked on the door, but he could plainly hear people talking and a TV playing inside. So he went to the back of the house, where he noticed that a gas grill was heating up. He hid behind some bushes, and when the tenant eventually came out to flip his burgers, he jumped like a commando from "Rent Team 6" and confronted the guy on the spot. Suffice it to say, the rent was eventually paid.

Jon is unusual (in more ways than one), because while some people enjoy conflicts over serious things like politics—or less serious things like "cats vs. dogs" or "Beatles vs. Stones"—most people don't. When it comes to being a landlord, who wouldn't prefer sipping a mai tai on the beach to text-fighting over the origins of a hole in the wall behind the sofa?

I mention this for one very important reason: In my experience, the main thing that keeps people from exploring Rent Estate isn't related to time, money, or risk. It's the fact that when you open the door to financial freedom, you also open the door to some level of dispute— especially as you add more properties and more tenants. In fact, you might say that success in Rent Estate is directly proportional to the potential for interpersonal conflict. (Notice I said "potential for," not "reality of," and that's important.)

For some people, this simple fact is a deal breaker. And that's too bad. Because in Rent Estate (as in life), conflict is inevitable. But it's also preventable. In practice, the human aspect of Rent Estate is actually one of its strongest benefits. Talk to successful Rent Estate investors who own multiple properties and have hosted dozens—even hundreds—of tenants over the years, and they'll tell you the same thing: The rewards far outweigh the conflicts.

Many property owners see the "people" aspect of Rent Estate as an opportunity to do good. Maybe they're empty-nesters who want to help young couples start a family in a great neighborhood. Maybe they're successful immigrants who want to help make the American Dream a reality for others like them. Maybe they know what it's like to struggle with college debt, and they want to provide a way for recent graduates to repair or build their credit.

Whatever the reason, Rent Estate's relationships separate it from the cold transactions of traditional buy-and-flip real estate. *People* are what make Rent Estate so special and rewarding—financially, emotionally, and, for some, even spiritually.

THE SKEPTIC SPEAKS

"That's all puppy dogs and rainbows, but you also said that disputes are inevitable. So what kinds of conflicts can I expect, and what can I do to address them?"

So much for my Kumbaya moment. Okay, let's talk about the most common types of conflicts you might experience in Rent Estate: late rent payments, damages, and evictions. I'll tell you how to deal with these areas. But even more important, I'll tell you how to *prevent* them.

Late Rent Payments

The first point of conflict that stresses out property owners is something I call FOLR: Fear of Late Rent. The repercussions of disrupted cash flow shouldn't be underestimated. After all, as a landlord, you count on revenue from monthly rent payments to cover your mortgage. So if your tenants can't pay, then neither can you—and banks tend to frown on that.

Unfortunately, one late or missed rent payment also has the potential to induce a financial domino effect. You might incur late charges and fees from the bank. You might have to transfer funds from a savings account that you promised never to touch. You might miss a deposit to a Roth IRA or other retirement account (which in turn reduces a potential tax write-off). And you might have to delay some important maintenance work on the property due to lack of funds.

> *"People* are what make Rent Estate so special and rewarding—financially, emotionally, and, for some, even spiritually."

A late rent payment can also be the first wave in a gradual erosion of trust between you and your tenants. And make no mistake: *Trust is your real currency.* When a tenant is late with rent, you can't help but wonder what else they might be neglecting. After all, if they don't respect your deadlines, how can they respect your property?

But let's talk about what most people really dread about late rent payments: having to play the bad cop. You want to trust people, not hound them. You want to be the Nice Guy Landlord, not the Harasser in Chief. You want stability in your tenant base, not the possibility of terminating or not renewing a lease (and then having to find new tenants). Most of all, you don't want to spend time begging for something you're already entitled to.

So in that spirit, here are four tips for minimizing FOLR—or better yet, preventing it from happening in the first place. Some of this advice dovetails with what we talked about in the previous chapter, but it's worth repeating.

1. Document everything.

The mantra of all real estate is "location, location, location," and the mantra of Rent Estate is "document, document, document." When it comes to rent, you need to spell out amounts, due dates, late fees, and other consequences *in writing*. The law is very clear on this. For example, if your lease doesn't specify that you *have* a late-rent fee—as well as how it's calculated and when it's triggered—then you can't impose one after the lease is signed.

After you specify the rent details in your lease agreement, you should have every adult who will be living in your property sign it, not just one. In fact, have everyone initial and date every page. Do the same yourself, then give copies to everyone. This provides evidence of clear communication and protects you if your tenants claim that they didn't know the ground rules.

2. Know the specific laws in your state and city.

When it comes to fees on late rent payments and bounced checks, the legal landscape is still a bit "Wild West." Every state's rules are different.

Whether you charge the full penalty allowed by law is your call. On one hand, charging in full discourages repeat offenders. On the other hand, you have to walk that fine line to keep trust intact.

Also keep in mind that if you come across a repeat offender, you can do more than charge late fees. You can also nick their credit score by reporting their late payments to the credit bureaus. But with this—as with all punitive actions—be sure to communicate the consequences ahead of time.

3. Feel like Kirk. Act like Spock.

Even the best renters can be forgetful or run into hard times. But no matter how much you might sympathize or emotionally identify with someone, it's important to keep your emotions in check and react to all situations in the most logical and predictable way possible.

Why? Because that old adage "give them an inch, and they'll take a mile" can apply to problem renters. In addition to developing a clear and reasonable late-rent policy, you need to exercise it consistently. Simply having the policy will incentivize most people to pay on time, but some will test you. If you respond to a late payment with something like "That's okay, just pay when you can," then you open a door you may never be able to close again.

Imposing consequences from the get-go sends the message that you mean business—not only on late fees, but on everything else in the lease. So think twice about forgiving a missed payment, delaying a late fee, or overlooking a bounced check. Unless you know that tenant extremely well, those decisions will come back to haunt you.

4. Outsource rent collection altogether.

The good news is, you don't have to worry about any of this. Because as you now know, rent collection is just one of the things that you can outsource to a professional property management firm.

We've already talked about the fact that outsourcing rent collection is more convenient for you and your tenants, but it also helps minimize conflicts. An effective property manager will make sure that rent terms and late fees are clearly spelled out in your lease agreements. They'll work to collect the rent for you and deposit it *in full* directly into your bank account. They'll keep tabs on when rent payments are late, notify tenants, and automatically impose any appropriate fees. What do you have to do? Nothing. Just relax. Be the good cop. Watch the money flow into your bank account every month. Better yet, research the next property to buy.

Damages to Your Property

Owning rental property means occasionally dealing with damages incurred by tenants, and this can be another sticky wicket. The first issue is, "What constitutes 'damages'?" After all, there's a certain amount of wear and tear that everyone—you, your tenants and a court of law—will consider normal. The second is, "Who's responsible for what in the first place?"

Properly maintaining a rental property is a cooperative effort in which both you and your tenants bear certain responsibilities. As a general rule, you're responsible for preventive maintenance; your tenants, are responsible for reporting problems. In other words: You need to make sure that the sump pump still works; your tenants need to tell you if water is seeping into the basement. The line between these two can be surprisingly fuzzy, and that's where problems can arise.

On the tenant side, make it clear that they need to report damages promptly. Make it easy for them to do, and make sure it's in writing. A phone call won't suffice. You need to require damage notifications via email, or offer an online form to fill out.

VIEW SAMPLE INSPECTION CHECKLISTS
@ RentEstateRevolution.com

On your end, start by making sure your tenants experience a proper inspection. This not only makes sure your property is "rent-ready"; it also eliminates the primary point of conflict when it comes to damages: a renter saying, "Hey, that carpet stain was already there!" It also addresses the wear-and-tear issue, which can get a little more complicated.

Make sure your property is up to code, and that you're always up to date on routine maintenance. That means regular inspections of multiple systems, depending on the property—fireplace, furnace, plumbing, and air-conditioning, to name a few. Systems inspections are like flu shots: Nothing more effectively prevents damage later on.

In addition, open that rainy-day account (1 to 2 percent of your property's value for annual maintenance) to cover maintenance and repair costs. Then do everything you can not to touch it. One of the best ways to do that is to follow these additional maintenance and damage-prevention tips:

1. Prioritize enhancements.

You may want to improve everything in your rental property at once, but that's usually not the smartest route to go. Run the numbers on things like replacing the kitchen floor, updating the plumbing, improving insulation, and adding solar panels to the roof. Then ask yourself: Which projects offer the best overall return on investment, and which ones will do the most to reduce tenant-related problems?

RENT ESTATE REMINDER
It might be tempting to go with inexpensive materials and fixes in a rental property, but that strategy usually comes back to bite you. Always have a "high-quality" mindset to avoid costlier issues later on.

---

2. Think guts, not skin.

It's tempting to focus on curb appeal and other superficial aspects of your property. These things look good on the surface and usually impress tenants when you're trying to land them. But once you actually have renters, the guts of the house matter most. Make sure your plumbing and electrical are up to code, your heating and cooling systems are functional and efficient, and all major appliances are in good working order.

"Keep exteriors on the functional side . . . focus on keeping driveways and walkways properly paved to avoid slip-and-falls."

---

3. Minimize "user error."

Most tenant damage happens to items that are in plain sight, so you need to prioritize these areas:

- **Countertops and Cabinets.** Going "heavy-duty" is usually worth the extra cost. For example, cabinets made out of real wood stand up better to daily tenant use. And maybe you can't afford fancy granite countertops, but going with a cheap laminate will cost you in the long run.

- **Doors.** Doors that don't function properly tend to invite damage through things like constant slamming and the forcing of locks. So make sure they fit properly and have functioning handles and lock systems. Also, invest in doorstops and wall bumpers to prevent scuffs in the walls.

- **Windows.** The same principle applies to windows. Make sure they slide easily, and close and lock properly. Check fail-safes, springs, and locks to make sure they won't break easily.

4. Keep the outside attractive but low-maintenance.

We'd all love to have a lush English garden, organic vegetable farm, and amusement park-quality water slide in the back yard. But in addition to being expensive to maintain, these kinds of amenities can also grossly increase your liability risks. As a rule, it's best to keep exteriors on the functional side. So forget about installing that zip line, and focus on keeping driveways and walkways properly paved to avoid slip-and-falls.

Evictions

We now arrive at the number-one fear of the nonconfrontational Rent Estate investor: having to kick out a tenant before the lease is up. Trust me, evictions don't happen often—especially if you follow the steps we've already outlined to find great tenants and minimize conflicts. But if you do get to the point of needing to evict someone, the truth is, it can get very messy, very quickly.

Let's start by taking a look at the entire eviction process. In general, it consists of four basic elements: Rent Collection, Eviction Hearings, Court Orders, and Writ/Lockout. Mapping them out from a professional property management company process standpoint, you get something like this:

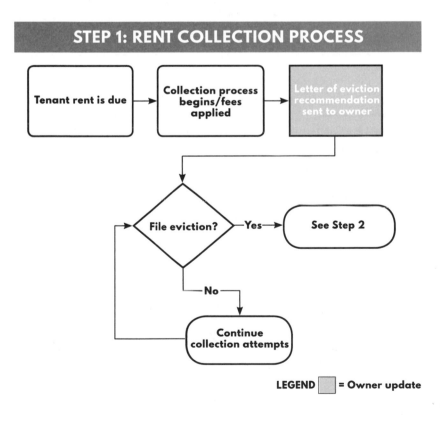

STEP 1: RENT COLLECTION PROCESS

Tenant rent is due → Collection process begins/fees applied → Letter of eviction recommendation sent to owner

File eviction? —Yes→ See Step 2

No → Continue collection attempts

LEGEND = Owner update

STEP 2: EVICTION HEARING PROCESS

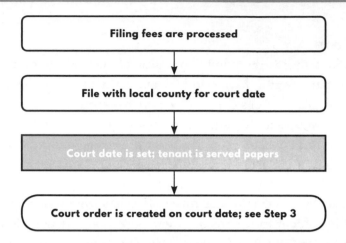

Filing fees are processed

File with local county for court date

Court date is set; tenant is served papers

Court order is created on court date; see Step 3

STEP 3: COURT ORDERS

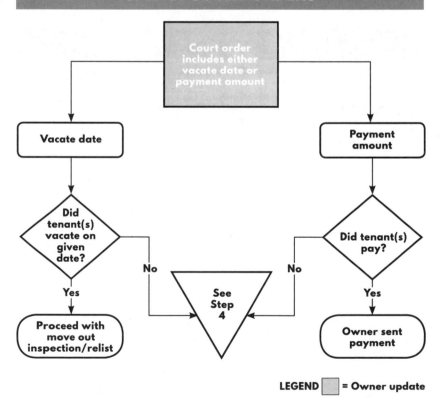

Court order includes either vacate date or payment amount

Vacate date

Payment amount

Did tenant(s) vacate on given date?

Did tenant(s) pay?

No — See Step 4 — No

Yes

Yes

Proceed with move out inspection/relist

Owner sent payment

LEGEND = Owner update

STEP 4: WRIT/LOCKOUT PROCESS

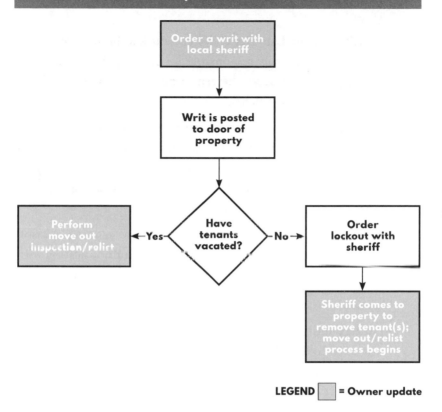

LEGEND ☐ = Owner update

Note how many of these elements involve unpleasant tasks on your part. *You* have to send the eviction notices. *You* have to file with the county for a court date. *You* have to order a writ with the sheriff.

And then there's the effect on your pocketbook. *You're* paying the court fees. And (assuming you hire a lawyer), *you're* shelling out the legal fees. If you handle rent collection and inspections yourself, you're also spending your precious hours harassing the tenant for late rent, as well as conducting the move-out inspection when they're gone. Sound like fun? I didn't think so. Once again, outsourcing to a professional property management firm is probably your best bet.

DIY Downsides/Outsourcing Upsides: The Art of Conflict

DIY Downsides

- **FOLR: Fear of Late Rent.** When you handle rent collection yourself, you're solely responsible for setting the terms, documenting the process, determining and enforcing late fees, and chasing down tenants.

- **Damages.** Without a professional property management firm running interference, you're on your own when it comes to inspections, maintenance schedules, fielding and documenting damage reports from your tenants, and getting everything fixed properly for the best price.

- **Evictions.** In a DIY world, you're the one sending eviction notices, filing paperwork with the county, communicating with the local sheriff, and paying legal and court fees.

Outsourcing Upsides

- **No late-rent chasing.** A good property management firm will not only collect the rent; they'll also help you set and collect appropriate late fees. You don't have to interact with your tenants *at all* over rent. You just get to appreciate the fact that someone else is paying your mortgage for you and building your equity in the property.

- **Damage prevention.** With a good property manager on your side, you avoid tenant damages in multiple ways. You have great tenants to begin with. The property is up to code and tenant-proofed. Inspections are properly handled and documented. Your lease agreements are crystal clear about who's responsible for maintenance issues. And you have a damage-reporting system in place that provides speedy communication and a valuable paper trail.

- **No nasty evictions.** A full-service property management firm should offer a comprehensive eviction service as an add-on product. This kind of service frees you from the headaches of awkward tenant confrontations, filling out reams of paperwork, navigating the justice system, and paying excessive legal costs.

RENT ESTATE RECAP

Three things in life are inevitable: death, taxes, and tenant conflicts. Having great renters to begin with prevents most of these problems and adds a rich layer of fulfillment to Rent Estate that you don't find with traditional real estate. But the best way to minimize tenant conflicts is to hire property-management professionals to handle things like rent collection, late fees, property damages, evictions, and paperwork for you.

---

3 TAKEAWAYS

1. Occasional tenant conflicts are inevitable, but overall, the "people" aspect of Rent Estate is one of its greatest assets.

2. A property management company can help prevent tenant conflicts in three common areas: late rent payments, damages to property, and evictions.

3. Freedom from tenant conflicts and legal fights makes Rent Estate work by enhancing your overall happiness and quality of life.

ACTION ITEM

Download the "9 Rental Property Disasters and How to Cope" guide at RentEstateRevolution.com.

SUMMARY

Unlike real estate, Rent Estate is essentially a people business. You don't need just any tenants; you need *great* tenants who consistently pay the rent and respect your property. Finding these renters used to be as simple as running a newspaper ad or posting on Craigslist. But in today's market, you need a comprehensive, customized digital marketing campaign.

Once you have great tenants, you need a sound strategy around managing the daily grind of collecting rent, doing inspections, trafficking maintenance calls, handling repairs, and avoiding potential legal issues. If you're a do-it-yourself type, then property management can quickly take over your life. But if you're not—or you just want to minimize conflicts over late rent, property damage, and evictions— then it's best to outsource some or all of these tasks to a professional property management firm.

Once you outsource your property management headaches, it's amazing what you *won't* have to do.

TOP 10 ANNOYING THINGS YOU WON'T HAVE TO DO WHEN YOU HIRE A PROFESSIONAL PROPERTY MANAGEMENT FIRM

1. Spend days going through endless tenant applications.

2. Spend weeks trying to replace a tenant.

3. Answer the phone at 2 A.M. about a clogged toilet.

4. Shake down a tenant who's late with the rent.

5. Confront a tenant who needs to be evicted.

6. Find out that the rent you're charging is too high to attract tenants, or too low to be profitable.

7. Get estimates from five different pest control companies about that roach infestation.

8. Fight with a tenant over their security deposit because you don't have proper inspection documentation.

9. Scramble to find that shoebox of receipts when it's time to do your taxes.

10. Miss your child's soccer game because you need to deal with another disgruntled tenant.

SECTION III

JOINING THE RENT ESTATE REVOLUTION

Well, we've landed. We've looked at Rent Estate from 30,000 feet. We've made our descent and surveyed the landscape of exactly what it involves. Now we're firmly on the ground and ready to navigate our way to our ultimate financial and lifestyle destination. But to reach that place, we need to pay attention and avoid making any wrong turns.

The fact that you've gotten this far tells me three things:

1. You truly care about retirement security, financial freedom, and achieving the New American Dream.

2. You recognize that in today's world, Rent Estate is the best way to achieve those things.

3. Now that you know everything it takes to own, rent, and manage residential real estate, your reaction is "Game on!"

That means you're ready for the nuts-and-bolts how-to information. My goal is to have you start researching residential investment properties immediately after you turn the last page of this book. So to help make that happen, I'm going to dive into the details of three important areas:

- Finding your first investment property
- Understanding Rent Estate terminology and numbers
- Building your empire

Once you have this information, you're ready to join the Rent Estate Revolution today and achieve financial freedom tomorrow. So let's do this.

CHAPTER 8

FINDING THAT FIRST PROPERTY

I once owned a property in Phoenix that lost more than half of its value during the Great Recession. Did I panic? No. Because it was a solid Rent Estate property, I had a great tenant, my loans were fixed, and I was confident that the market would bounce back. Which it did.

I mention this because when it comes to finding a Rent Estate property, you need to start with an old-fashioned idea: *patience*. This is a trait we don't value so much in our attention-deficit society anymore. (When have you ever heard a late-night TV infomercial offering a surefire way to "get rich slow"?) But in Rent Estate, patience is not only a virtue; it's a lucrative business mindset.

In real estate, buy-and-flip schemes depend on timing the market. If you buy a property and bet on values to rise within a certain time frame, then it'd better happen. Otherwise, you're forced to sell prematurely, and you can lose a lot of money. Rent Estate is different. It frees you to take a deep breath, because it's the long game—the difference between building a consistently great football team like the New England Patriots vs. playing one-day fantasy football.

Lots of successful Rent Estate investors started with properties that delivered negative cash flow for a few years. In other words, what they initially collected in rent didn't even cover the mortgage, property taxes, and other expenses on the property. But they knew the neighborhood, the market, and the bigger economic trends. So eventually they were able to raise rents and clear hundreds of dollars every month. All it took was a little patience.

If you want to gamble on making a quick buck, then buy-and-flip real estate is for you. But if you'd rather build wealth under the proven adage that "slow and steady wins the race," then you're a good fit for Rent Estate.

Applying the Four Pillars

Considering any Rent Estate investment property means going back to the Four Pillars of Financial Freedom we discussed in Chapter 3, "Rent Estate = Financial Freedom." To evaluate a single-family rental, you can apply each pillar as a question:

1. Will this property deliver positive long-term **cash flow?**
2. Will I be able to build **equity** in this property as a rental?
3. Is this property likely to **appreciate** in value?
4. Will this property consistently offer excellent **tax breaks** every April 15?

If you can confidently answer "yes" to all of these, then the property is probably a good Rent Estate investment. But let me ask you an even more fundamental question, because when it comes to finding your *first* Rent Estate property, this issue represents the most significant fork in the road:

Do you currently own a home?

Your answer to this will set you on the right Rent Estate path from the beginning. So let's consider both the "yes" fork and the "no" fork in answering this question.

Fork #1: "Yes, I currently own a home."

If you have a mortgage, then you have a business. You're already a Rent Estate Entrepreneur-in-waiting, and you didn't even know it. Maybe this thought excites you. Maybe it scares you a little. But the sooner you embrace it, the better off you'll be.

The point is, you might already own the best property to rent. The next question is "Are you willing to move out and turn it into a rental?"

**THE SKEPTIC
SPEAKS**

"I've heard your company's catchy jingle, and one of the lines is 'don't sell, rent instead.' So don't you already believe that everyone who owns a home should rent it out?"

I agree that our jingle is an ear worm, but I disagree on the "rent bias" point. If you're a homeowner, then you should definitely *consider* renting, but it's not an automatic decision. Yes, your best first rental property is probably right under your nose. But I say "probably" for a good reason, because you need to look seriously at the pros and cons.

On the pro side, renting your existing home is almost always easier than starting from scratch. The financing is already in place. You've already built some equity. You know the house inside and out. You have a good sense of whether the neighborhood is on its way up or down. And since time is money, you can save thousands of dollars by *not* having to research and assess other properties.

The cons of renting can be both practical and emotional. Maybe you're content where you are, and you just don't want to move. Maybe your house has been in the family for generations or has other sentimental value. Perhaps the plan has always been to stay until you and your spouse reach "empty-nest syndrome." These reasons are completely valid and understandable. After all, is there any property that carries more emotional value than a family home?

On the other hand, maybe your house won't make a great rental. Maybe you can't legally rent it due to zoning restrictions or home-owners association rules. Maybe it has quirks that you've learned to tolerate but that would likely bother a renter (like poor heating, super-creaky steps, or a tiny kitchen). Maybe the house is high maintenance due to extensive landscaping needs or a backyard pool. Or maybe the rent would simply be too high to attract tenants.

Sometimes the issue isn't with your house, but with the neighbor-hood. Are there other rentals on your block? If not, that might tell you something. Maybe the area is too noisy, or crime is on the rise. Maybe it isn't close enough to big employers, public transit, good schools, or that popular new bike path.

If some or all of this is the case, then by all means stay where you are and look elsewhere for your first Rent Estate property. But if your home and neighborhood are renter friendly, then the next issue is purely economic: "In the long run, can I get more money out of my home by selling it or renting it?"

The Economics of Renting vs. Selling

The first step in finding out whether selling or renting your home will be more lucrative is figuring out how much you should charge in rent. As I've said previously, part of this decision is driven by marketing. You're looking for the number that reflects your home's *real* value but that will also attract good tenants without pricing them out. Remember: A rental home without tenants not only produces zero cash flow; it can also start to decline in value.

RENT ESTATE REMINDER
Unless you're selling your house on your own, don't forget to factor in commissions and closing costs on a sale. That 8% can really gut your profit.

Now, here's where a lot of people miss the boat. Once you have that monthly rent number, your knee-jerk reaction is to grab the nearest napkin and do some quick math. Unfortunately, it's almost always the *wrong* math. And bad arithmetic is the number-one reason why people miss out on making money in Rent Estate.

At Renters Warehouse, we've captured this "right math/wrong math" challenge in something we call "The Back of the Napkin Test." Here's a summary of how bad math usually plays out in evaluating your home's true worth:

> "Zillow says my house is worth $200,000.
> My mortgage is at $175,000. So subtract the
> two, and I can clear $25,000 on a sale."

That's a decent number, and you can't help but imagine a check for $25,000 flying right into your wallet. Then you consider renting, and the conventional logic goes like this:

> "I'm guessing that I can rent my place for about
> $1,350. Minus mortgage, insurance, and taxes, that
> leaves $220 a month, or $2,640 a year. So $25,000
> right now, or $2,640 a year from now. I should sell."

When you look at it that way, selling *does* seem better. But guess what? It's not. In fact, it's not even close. The real math will show you all the reasons why, including these:

- The napkin math doesn't take commissions and closing costs into account on a sale. Those are usually around 8%, so that guts your profit on a sale from $25,000 down to just **$9,000**.

- In just 7 years of cash flow alone, you actually make twice as much money—**$18,480**—by renting vs. doing a one-and-done sale. That grows to over **$26,000** in 10 years, and to over **$79,000** in 30 years.

- When you factor in equity and appreciation, by the time you do sell the house some 30 years later, your total profit balloons to **$565,000**—and that's being conservative.

- We haven't even touched on the thousands of dollars you've also saved on taxes by renting. That's the cherry on top.

So in looking at selling vs. renting in this example (which is pretty typical), it's not "$25,000 vs. $2,640." It's actually "$9,000 vs. nearly $565,000." All it takes is a little patience.

Of course, this is a generic scenario. Your house and your situation are unique, and you'll need to consider several factors in determining whether renting or selling is better for you. The result can hinge on the current value of your home, how much you still owe on it, your interest rate, how much rent you could charge, and how much you would have to pay in commissions and fees on a sale—among other things.

FOR A TWO-MINUTE VIDEO VERSION SHOWING HOW TO DO THE REAL MATH, WATCH OUR VIDEO "BACK OF THE NAPKIN TEST" @ RentEstateRevolution.com

Fork #2: "I don't own a home, so I need to start from scratch."

If you're just beginning the process of finding your first rental property, then your overall goal is to pay below market value for a low-maintenance property in a solid (and up-and-coming, but not too ritzy) neighborhood. That's a given, but other principles apply as well, so here are your Top 5 Strategies for Buying a Successful First Rent Estate Property.

1. **Work with an agent—but not just any agent.**

   As with finding a home to live in, locating rental property is much easier if you work with a real estate agent. But here's the thing: Not all agents are created equal. While any residential real estate professional is well trained in listing property, only a select few also understand the investment side of the equation. We call this "being Rent Estate savvy."

   At Renters Warehouse, we're dedicated to boosting Rent Estate acumen through extensive training in the field. In fact, we're building a Rent Estate certification program to teach real estate agents how to help people find residential investment property by knowing how to navigate the Multiple Listing Service (MLS), as well as the wide array of single-family rental online marketplaces. Someday soon, you'll hopefully be able to find an agent who's also "Rent Estate Certified."

   The right real estate agent will help you address all the important factors when it comes to finding a good home to rent: How's the neighborhood? Are businesses closing, moving, opening up, expanding? Are nearby schools adding new buildings and increasing enrollment? Is crime declining or on the rise? Is the city investing in high-speed buses and light rail in the area? Is the old Blockbuster now an organic restaurant, or a payday loan provider?

   But a Rent Estate–savvy agent can also do quite a bit more for you. They can find the quality and consistency in homes and neighborhoods that you need. They can do a comparative market analysis, which tells you the prices that similar properties in the same area recently sold for. They can find properties with lower long-range costs based on age and other factors. And they can offer sound advice on whether you should consider properties like foreclosures, fixer-uppers, and auctions.

Finally (plug alert): Renters Warehouse offers a nice referral fee for real estate agents who refer investment clients to us for property management. So if you're in the business or know someone who is, find the details at rerterswarehouse.com. :)

2. Leverage other people's money.

Like any investment, Rent Estate essentially comes down to trying to make a lot of money by putting in very little—minimizing your personal investment while reaping the rewards of future growth. In the next chapter, "Rent Estate by the Numbers," we'll get into the details of how to evaluate Rent Estate property and measure a rental home's financial performance. But the most important point is this: Rent Estate requires far less cash to get started than you probably think.

In fact, Rent Estate is absolutely amazing in its ability to let you play with other people's money. As I've said before and will continue to repeat: Rent Estate is one of the only investments you can make using borrowed cash. Banks have a high degree of confidence that they'll make money on those loans, and that tells you everything you need to know about the power and stability of real estate investments over time.

When it comes to leverage, an added benefit is the world of loans insured by the Federal Housing Administration (FHA). We'll talk more about these in Chapter 10, "Growing Your Rent Estate Empire," but the overview is this: A byproduct of efforts to stem the Great Depression is the fact that you can secure home loans backed by the FHA that require very little money down. As a Rent Estate investor, you can buy properties using these loans—including two- to four-unit properties—as long as you carry only one FHA loan at a time and live in the property.

3. Don't be scared by negative cash flow. A $200 monthly loss is just like putting $200/month into your 401(k).

The Great Recession left a lot of homeowners in the cold—sometimes literally. But for residential real estate investors, it also produced some wildly unrealistic expectations. Yes, there was a time when you could scoop up a fabulous single-family home in a great neighborhood at a rock-bottom auction price, and then either flip it for a quick profit or clear $800 a month by renting it.

Those days have largely passed. The problem is, they've also left a lingering expectation for great bargains and immediate gratification. If you expect huge Rent Estate gains on day one, then you might not consider a property that produces negative initial cash flow. That's too bad, because you might be missing out on huge profits in the long term.

If you (or your Rent Estate–savvy agent) do your homework, then you'll always recognize a promising home with a bright rental future. In other words, lots of properties won't produce enough rental income right away to cover your mortgage and other expenses. But as you're able to raise the rent, some will turn profitable after just one, two, or three years.

If you can afford to take a small hit for a short time, then definitely do so if the long-term forecast calls for an appreciating property that will deliver increasing monthly cash flow. Think of your property like you think of a 401(k) or other investment account. Investing in it every month is to be expected. The amazing thing about Rent Estate is that when you reach positive monthly cash flow, in addition to paying in to your investment, your investment pays *you*.

4. Buy a property with two to four units, such as a duplex.[1]

If you remember my story from the introduction, you'll recall that my own Rent Estate journey started with purchasing a single modest duplex in the Phoenix area while I was a student at Arizona State University. Buying that property seemed like a no-brainer at the time, because by occupying one unit and renting out the other, I was able to live rent-free for the duration of college. Not only that, I was actually able to clear a small profit every month.

Over time, I realized that buying that duplex was an even smarter decision than I thought. Physically living in your rental property not only saves money; it also makes it easier to relate to your tenants, address maintenance issues, and prevent problems. After all, it's a lot harder for a tenant to be late with the rent when they see their landlord at the mailbox every day. And if you literally live above, below, or next to your tenants, you can address an issue like loud music before it escalates.

Finally, remember what we said about "other people's money"? Duplexes, triplexes, and fourplexes make leverage especially easy. FHA loans can apply to residential buildings of up to four units (as long as you live in one of them for a period of time). But also, if you're cash-strapped and especially light on down-payment funds, you can actually use *potential rent from the other unit* to help qualify for a bank loan.

Especially if you're in your 20s and currently live in an apartment, I would highly recommend that you make your foray into Rent Estate by buying a duplex, triplex, or fourplex and moving into one of the units. These multi-unit buildings are a great way to save money for additional Rent Estate properties down the line.

---

1   *Single-family rental* means not only houses but any residential property up to four units.

5. Join your local real estate investment club.

Every major American city contains a core group of real estate investor clubs. These groups can be tremendously useful in helping you learn about the area, find leads on promising investment property, and tap local resources for financing, maintenance, repair, and property management issues. Start by visiting the website of the National Real Estate Investors Association (www.nationalreia.org). From there, you can find local associations all over the country.

We've actually set up a "Rent Estate Club" at Renters Warehouse, because we think Rent Estate done right is like having a membership to a subscription-based service. Realizing that outsourcing property management helps you build your Rent Estate Empire is the key to successful wealth creation, retirement security, and financial freedom.

RENT ESTATE RECAP

Making the right call on your first investment property is key to building your Rent Estate Empire. If you already own a home and aren't bent on keeping it for the rest of your life, then your best bet is probably to rent it instead of selling it. But if you're starting from scratch, then you should work with a Rent Estate–savvy real estate agent to locate the best property. Keep in mind that buying Rent Estate isn't a get-rich-quick scheme. It's a long-term decision based on a property's *potential* to produce increasing rental income while also appreciating in value and delivering tax benefits.

3 TAKEAWAYS

1. You might get more value out of your home by turning it into Rent Estate vs. selling it.

2. In trying to decide whether to sell or rent your home, the *real* math factors long-term cash flow, equity, appreciation, and tax breaks into the equation.

3. Your mother was right: patience is a virtue. Just as you put money into a 401(k) every month, a Rent Estate property is a monthly investment in a historically appreciating asset.

ACTION ITEM

Download "The Handbook to Renting vs. Selling Your Home" at RentEstateRevolution.com.

CHAPTER 9

RENT ESTATE BY THE NUMBERS

We've talked about the human side of Rent Estate; now it's time for a deeper dive into the numbers side. I don't know about you, but I was never taught the basics of money when I was growing up. Not in elementary school. Not in high school. Not ever.

I'm guessing that I'm not alone in this deficiency, because our country's financial literacy leaves something to be desired. That might be the reason why 56 percent of us have less than $10,000 saved for retirement.[1]

The point is this: To take full advantage of everything Rent Estate has to offer, you need to know the numbers. You need a snapshot of how Rent Estate compares with other investments on several key fronts, and you need a basic understanding of its financial terminology. An entire book could be dedicated to this subject alone, but I'm going to give you the "Kevin's Notes" version.

Before we jump in, a side note: No matter how many experts and consultants you work with, your success in Rent Estate is ultimately up to *you*. Others may do the research and crunch the numbers for you, but it's your responsibility to understand the information and use it to make good decisions.

---

1   Elyssa Kirkham, "1 in 3 Americans Has Saved $0 for Retirement," *Money*, May 14, 2016, http://time.com/money/4258451/retirement-savings-survey/.

The good news is, this stuff isn't that hard! When all is said and done, you don't need an MBA to understand Rent Estate; you just need a calculator.

Rent Estate vs. Other Investments

When it comes to personal finance, what's the most common word you hear? *Diversify!*

That's sound advice. But today, diversification means more than just buying stocks and bonds, opening up a Roth IRA, and starting an annuity. It means investing in Rent Estate (if I do say so myself). I'm not saying that Rent Estate should be the only thing you invest in, but it should definitely be a part of your portfolio. As one example, consider the obvious benefits of Rent Estate vs. a 401(k).

	401(k)	Rent Estate
Has the potential to provide immediate cash flow without penalty.		✓
Designed to create long-term wealth through appreciation.	✓	✓
You can borrow money from a bank to invest in it.		✓
Delivers tax benefits.	✓	✓
Depends on regular financial contributions.	✓	✓
Those contributions are made by other people, not you.		✓
Provides a strong hedge against inflation.		✓

Now, let's look at Rent Estate through four lenses that play a big role in any investment: performance, accessibility, inflation, and taxes. I think you'll agree that when you compare Rent Estate to many other options, it's not only better; it's more accessible for regular people like us.

Performance

The world of real estate can seem risky, but history shows that Rent Estate is a reliably favorable investment. All investments experience variations in performance. But the data show that single-family rentals can outperform stocks over the long haul. (After all, there must be a reason why banks will lend you money for real estate and not equities: They know they're much more likely to get their money back on a real estate investment.)

Plus, real estate delivers amazingly consistent returns. While the stock market fluctuates between boom and bust, real estate prices in America have risen since World War II at a steady average of 5 percent a year.[2]

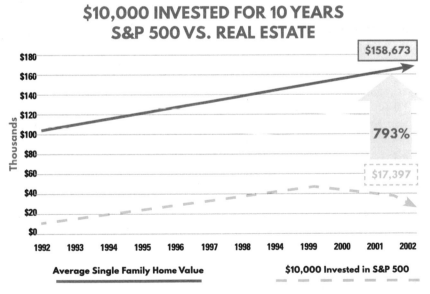

Source: *JasonHartman.com*

---

2   Janet Portman, "What It's Like Being a Landlord," *Nolo*, www.nolo.com/legal-encyclopedia/landlord-pros-cons-29494.html.

Greater Accessibility

By "accessibility," I'm talking about capital—as in, "How much money do I need to enter the Rent Estate market?" All investment opportunities require money to get started. There's no free lunch. But this is where we can bust one of the biggest myths about Rent Estate, and I'm happy to do so.

Conventional wisdom says that it's relatively easy to enter the stock market. As of this writing, a single share in Target is priced at about $72. That sounds highly accessible in theory, and plenty of websites will help you buy it. Plus, your place of employment probably has a 401(k) plan that's tied to the stock market, and some companies automatically enroll you when you're hired. Easy peasy, right? All it takes to enter the stock market is getting a job or making a few clicks on a website.

Buying real estate is a different story. Even if we're talking about a single-family home, you need tens of thousands of dollars for a down payment, and that's capital intensive. Plus, every time you buy more property, you need the same amount of cash or more, right?

Not so fast. Prior to writing this book, I bought a duplex using a process that proves how little money you need to get started in Rent Estate. Here's how it worked:

- I secured an FHA loan for $100,000.
- I bought the building for $70,000 with only $1,500 down.
- I spent the other $30,000 rehabbing the property.
- After the renovation, the property was worth $150,000.

That's one example, but the Rent Estate market is filled with them. Rent Estate is "real estate for the rest of us" for a reason. If you already own a home, you're already on your way. But even if you don't, the capital you need to get started is probably lower than you think. As we'll discover in the next chapter, you can realistically fund your entire retirement with just $5,000 properly invested in Rent Estate.

A Better Hedge Against Inflation

When comparing investment vehicles, inflation is probably the second-most underrated factor that people fail to take into account. (Spoiler alert: Number one is taxes, which we'll cover next.)

Think about this: The interest rate on your savings account is probably so low—and your fees so high—that you're actually losing money on it. And while equity markets do tend to go up over time, stock values aren't directly linked to inflation in quite the same way as real estate.

> "[Rent Estate] is the ideal scenario for an investor: The money coming in can rise with inflation; the money going out stays the same."

And then there's Rent Estate. When it comes to *really* protecting you against the financial erosion of inflation, nothing beats owning rental property. Rent Estate delivers three distinct advantages that collectively provide an incredibly strong hedge against rising prices:

1. The rent you charge is flexible.
2. Your mortgage payments are fixed.
3. The value of your property rises to reflect inflation.

As a Rent Estate investor, you can always raise rents in accordance with your lease terms, and you can do so to reflect both your property's rising value *and* the general rate of inflation. But assuming you were smart and signed a 30-year fixed mortgage, your payments to the bank are never going to change. It's the ideal scenario for an investor: The money coming in can rise with inflation; the money going out stays the same.

Because of this, your cash flow tends to increase over time—which also means that you can speed up the purchase of another investment property. You might even reach Rent Estate's magic moment: the day when your mortgage is completely paid off, but rent payments are still flowing into your bank account every month. *Ka-ching!*

> ## RENT ESTATE REMINDER
> You can deduct up to $25,000 in losses on your taxes if your modified adjusted gross income is $100,000 or less. While you can't depreciate the value of the land itself, you can deduct some of the lost value that occurs through depreciation.

A Decisive Tax Advantage[3]

Taxes are an X factor in any investment scenario. But when it comes to the almighty IRS, Rent Estate delivers some incredible advantages that make it quite attractive. And as I said earlier, this is the number-one element of Rent Estate that most people overlook.

Here's a simple comparison. With stocks, you have to pay capital gains tax on any profits you make from selling them. Even if you don't sell, you have to pay taxes on your dividends. With Rent Estate, you obviously have to pay property taxes, as well as taxes on your rental income. But if you think that sounds like a big hit, think again. In actual practice, your tax burden with Rent Estate can be surprisingly minimal. Here's why:

> ### As a Rent Estate Entrepreneur, you can deduct the majority of your expenses.

That's right. Whereas the only thing you can deduct on the home you live in is probably your mortgage interest, Rent Estate delivers loads of additional tax breaks. In fact, when you add up all your tax

---

3   Always work with a licensed tax professional to help you navigate the tax advantages of real estate investment.

deductions on an individual property, you can often claim a loss, which can save hundreds—even thousands—of dollars.

Here's a list of Rent Estate's many substantial tax deductions:

Property Manager Fees
This is ultimately what makes Rent Estate such a no-brainer: When you hire a professional property manager, you can use those fees as a write-off. At Renters Warehouse, our tenant placement and management fees are tax deductible.

Maintenance
Reasonable repairs to your rental properties are tax deductible in the year they occur, including painting, some plumbing, and fixing drywall, doors/locks, and broken windows.[4]

Advertising
Any reasonable fee you pay to advertise your property can be partially or fully expensed.

Depreciation
You can deduct a certain percentage of your property through lost-value depreciation. Property that wears out, decays, gets used up, or becomes obsolete over time qualifies for depreciation. Unfortunately, the federal government doesn't count land itself as a depreciating asset, so it's not included in this deduction.

Travel
Any travel to or from local or long-distance rental properties can be expensed as mileage. This amount changes every year, but it's generally around $0.54/mile.

---

4   Note: Replace items with others of the same quality. "Upgrades" are considered improvements, and may not qualify for tax deductions.

Interest

You can deduct the interest on your mortgage or the interest on credit card expenses used for management purposes. Mortgage interest is often the single largest deduction you can make.

Insurance

The premiums you pay for your property can be deducted, including fire, theft, flood, and liability insurance.

Legal and Professional Services

You can deduct legal, accounting, and real estate investment advisor fees as operating expenses.

Believe me, this all adds up quickly. And every April, you'll be happy it does.

Rent Estate Terminology: Assessment

Now that we've compared Rent Estate to other investments, let's dive into the unique language around it. Some of these terms will already be familiar to you, but take a close look at all of them. The sooner you speak *Rent Estate*, the faster you'll be able to profit from it.

Price Per Square Foot

This is the Clydesdale of real estate terminology—the workhorse. The calculation is simple, and I'm sure you're already familiar with it:

$$\textbf{Asking Price} \div \textbf{Total Square Footage} = \textbf{Price Per Square Foot}$$

For example, if you're looking at purchasing a $200,000 single-family rental that has 1,500 square feet of livable space, then your price per square foot is simply:

$$\$200,000 \div 1,500 = \$133.33$$

Perhaps the most useful application of price-per-square-foot calculations is in comparing the affordability of real estate in different markets. The best values are usually in mid-level metro areas. For example, the average price per square foot of a residence in Manhattan's Central Park South neighborhood recently hit a jaw-dropping $2,521.[5] By comparison, the number in my hometown of Minneapolis currently sits at a much more affordable $168.[6]

Price-to-Rent Ratio

This number is generally used by consumers to determine whether a housing market is more favorable for buying a home or renting one. It's calculated as follows:

Asking Price of Home ÷ Cost of Renting for 1 Year = Price-to-Rent Ratio

So for a $150,000 home in Kansas City that would rent for $1,300/month, you get:

$150,000 ÷ $15,600 = 9.61

A middle-ground price-to-rent number is typically somewhere between 15 and 20. In general, numbers higher than 20 say, "This is a rental market," while ones that are lower than 15 say, "This is a buyers' market." By way of comparison, recent price-to-rent ratios were 46 in San Francisco and only 6 in Detroit.[7] People who are looking for a home to live in are much more likely to rent in San Francisco and buy in Detroit.

As a Rent Estate investor, you'll find price-to-rent ratios useful in a couple of ways. First, if you're considering renting out your

5   "Priciest NYC Neighborhood by Square Foot? It's Central Park South," Streeteasy, January 11, 2016, http://streeteasy.com/blog/priciest-nyc-neighborhoods-by-square-foot/.

6   "Find Your Ideal Neighborhood," Realtor.com, http://www.realtor.com/local/55406.

7   Based on U.S. Census Data, https://smartasset.com/mortgage/price-to-rent-ratio-in-us-cities.

current home, this ratio can tell you at a glance whether your property is likely to appeal to consumers as a rental. Second, these numbers can help you locate great markets in which to buy rental property.

That said, it's important to keep one thing in mind when it comes to price-to-rent ratios. It's not as simple as saying, "The higher the ratio, the better the market for me to buy residential real estate." Overheated markets like Silicon Valley are insanely competitive and may have reached their rental plateau. Buying a rental property in San Jose is like buying a stock at its historically most expensive price. You have to ask yourself, "Is there any upside left?" Probably not. For that reason, a middle market like St. Louis—with a price-to-rent-ratio around 17—is probably a better place to look.[8]

Rent Estate Terminology: Operations

It's one thing to figure out whether to buy a manufacturing plant that churns out widgets; it's another to determine whether the plant is going to make money once it's operational. So far, we've looked at Rent Estate terms that apply more to assessing the overall value of a particular property or geographic market before you buy it. Now let's talk about terms related to how lucrative a property might be once it's actually in operation.

Making this kind of assessment requires a deep dive into all the factors that ultimately determine your Rent Estate return on investment (ROI). Remember, you're running a business here, so this is about measuring both earnings and costs.

Gross Income and Effective Gross Income

You're in the business of Rent Estate, so "income" refers to the rental income you generate (or can reasonably expect to generate) from the tenants in your rental property. In this case, you'll want to look at an annual number, which is simply:

Monthly Rental Income x 12 = Gross Income

However—and this is important—you can't assume that your properties will always be occupied. Turnover is inevitable. So, as in commercial real estate, you need to take a vacancy rate into account. Doing this gives you a more realistic and meaningful number, called effective gross income.

For single-family rentals, a typical standard vacancy rate is 5 percent[9], or slightly more than one month of vacancy every two years. Factoring that into the gross income generated by a home that you rent out for $1,300/month, you get:

$$
\begin{aligned}
\$1,300 \times 12 &= \$15,600 \\
-\$15,600 \times 5\% &= \$780 \\
\hline
\text{Effective Gross Income} &= \$14,820
\end{aligned}
$$

Don't be overly optimistic in choosing your vacancy rate number. No matter how attractive your property is as a rental, it'll sometimes sit idle.

Operating Expenses

Now let's move to the "cost" side of the ledger. As you might expect, operating expenses include every dollar it takes to run your rental property business. But one thing might surprise you: *In Rent Estate, operating expenses don't include your mortgage payments.*

I'll tell you where those go in a bit, but it's important to get this across now, because it can become a psychological barrier for some people: Your mortgage payments aren't expenses any more

9   Brian Honea, "SFR Vacancy Rate Levels Off After Months of Rising," *MReport*, November 1, 2016, http://www.themreport.com/daily-dose/11-01-2016/sfr-vacancy-rate-levels-months-rising.

than your 401(k) contributions are. They're helping you to *own* your property, not operate it.

Rent Estate operating expenses do, however, include the following, so don't leave any of these out of the equation:

- Property taxes
- Insurance payments
- Utilities (unless paid by the tenant)
- Repairs and maintenance (landscaping, lawn care, trash and snow removal)
- Property management fees
- Fees paid to attorneys or accountants

Net Operating Income (NOI)

Now that we've covered both revenue and expenses, we can narrow our focus down to the actual amount of cash that your Rent Estate property can generate when all is said and done—and begin to look at real rates of return on your investment.

NOI is a way of figuring out how much revenue your Rent Estate property will generate, without taking mortgage payments into account. So it's basically your rental income minus your operations costs, or:

Effective Gross Income – Operating Expenses = Net Operating Income

Going back to our house in Kansas City that rents for $1,300/month, let's say that house carries various operating expenses that total $3,000/year. In that case, your annualized NOI looks like this:

$14,820 – $3,000 = $11,820

Bottom line: You know that your Rent Estate property generates a net of almost $12,000 a year in cash. And that number will come into play often.

Capitalization Rate

Now that you know your property's NOI, the next question is: "What kind of annual return can I expect on my investment in this property?" In real estate, that's called the capitalization rate, or "cap rate." In a nutshell, the cap rate tells you your annual return on a property by looking at the income it generates, divided by the original sale price you bought it for:

$$\text{NOI} \div \text{Purchase Price} = \text{Cap Rate}$$

You purchased that $1,300/month rental home in Kansas City for $150,000, so your cap rate calculation looks like this:

$$\$11,820 \div \$150,000 = 7.9\% \text{ Cap Rate}$$

Keep in mind that this calculation doesn't take *appreciation* into account—one of our four pillars of financial freedom. Your property's value is likely rising in the background, so you should be able to increase your revenue by raising the rent over time.

The other thing about cap rates—and this is why I'm not crazy about using them in Rent Estate—is this: They assume that you paid for your property entirely in cash. Most Rent Estate investors don't do that, nor should they.

So if you have leveraged money invested in your Rent Estate property, then you need a different kind of calculation to get an accurate picture of how well your investment will perform. Luckily, just such a calculation exists. It's called "cash-on-cash return."

To figure out your cash-on-cash return, we need to finally add those mortgage payments into the equation. Which brings me to debt service.

Debt Service

This one is easy. Debt service is just a fancy term for your mortgage payment. It has nothing to do with property taxes, even if you fold those into your monthly payment. It's simply the sum of your principal and interest payment, period.

Cash-on-Cash Return

We now arrive at cash-on-cash return—the most important number in Rent Estate. If you did pay cash for your property (as the cap rate calculation assumes), then you don't need to bother finding your cash-on-cash return. It's the same as your cap rate.

But if the amount of actual cash that you invested in your Rent Estate property was just a fraction of the asking price, then we have to measure the cash you put into the property vs. the cash you're earning on it.

Put simply, cash-on-cash return is "cash in vs. cash out"—the net amount of money your property generates divided by the money you put into it in the form of your down payment. So:

$$\frac{\text{NOI - Debt Service (Cash In)}}{\text{Down Payment (Cash Out)}} = \text{Cash-on-Cash Return \%}$$

In our ongoing example, let's say the debt service on your Rent Estate property is $750 a month, or $9,000 a year. Your total annual "cash in" is then $2,820 (NOI minus debt service). Then let's say your down payment was the standard 20 percent, or $30,000. That gives you a cash-on-cash return as follows:

$$\$2,820 \div \$30,000 = 9.4\%$$

That's a more accurate rate of return on your Rent Estate property. And when you compare it to the anemic (or nonexistent) returns you might be seeing on your savings account, you can see why Rent Estate is such an awesome investment opportunity. But keep in mind: Because cash-on-cash return doesn't take appreciation or tax benefits into account, it still *understates* the total financial potential of your Rent Estate investment.

RENT ESTATE RECAP

Rent Estate has incredible power to outperform other investments on several fronts—including stability, accessibility, tax advantages, and the fact that it's an excellent hedge against inflation. But to know if any individual property is worthy of your Rent Estate portfolio, you need to become fluent in the language of gross income, operating expenses, cash-on-cash return, and other important terms related to Rent Estate appraisal, performance, and profitability.

---

3 TAKEAWAYS

1. Rent Estate investments are an excellent way to diversify your investment portfolio.

2. Rent Estate delivers multiple tax breaks and can reduce your personal income on tax filings—putting more money in your pocket.

3. The true return on a Rent Estate investment is best measured in a cash-on-cash return, which compares the money you put down to the net cash the property will generate in rental income.

ACTION ITEM

Download our "Primary Tax Advantages Gained from Rent Estate" guide at RentEstateRevolution.com.

CHAPTER 10

GROWING YOUR RENT ESTATE EMPIRE

I've said throughout this book that Rent Estate is remarkably accessible for regular folks. Now I'd like to prove it. First I'm going to walk through a example of how someone with a small amount of cash can use Rent Estate to achieve financial freedom. Then we'll go back and look in more depth at the elements that go into doing this for yourself.

Financial Freedom for Just $5,000

Even if you only have a few thousand dollars to invest, Rent Estate gives you an amazing opportunity to grow that investment with minimal risk. That's because Rent Estate delivers the unique ability to build yourself a financial freedom machine: With a modest amount of upfront capital, Rent Estate generates its own cash—which can fuel additional investments.

To demonstrate this, let's focus on a fictional character named "Tracy." Tracy only has $5,000 to invest, so any further investments must be made using money directly generated from Rent Estate. This example will show how Tracy can set herself up for a wonderful retirement by making just **6** property buys over the next **10 years**.

Year 1: First Purchase

At the start of our story, Tracy lives in an apartment and pays $950 a month in rent. But this is all about to change, because she buys a $142,000 duplex using an FHA loan—which only requires a 3.5 percent down payment, or $4,970.

Right off the bat, Tracy is saving about **$750** a month from when she was just shelling out rent. That's because her new monthly mortgage expenses are about $1,000, but she's living in one unit and renting the other one out for $800 a month. She's paying a net of $200/month, whereas she used to spend $950/month in rent (so $950 – $200 = $750). Even after Tracy pays a professional property management company and establishes a maintenance reserve, she's still able to save over **$6,000** a year.

Because she's a smart investor, Tracy puts all the money she's saving into an account (call it her "Rent Estate Acquisition Fund," or REAF) so she can buy more rental properties. Because she has a property manager doing all her grunt work, she's free to work her day job without distraction, as well as keep an eye out for her next property.

Year 4: Second Purchase

After three years living in the duplex with a renter in the other unit, Tracy has now saved over $18,000. She has also found a promising single-family rental for $90,000, so the money she's saved from the duplex covers her 20 percent down payment.

When she does the math on the house, she finds that she can rent it for $900 a month and clear over **$400** in positive cash flow. Even with outsourced property management and her usual maintenance reserve, this property now brings in about **$2,700** a year in profit. So she adds it to the REAF.

Year 7: Third Purchase

By continuing to bank over $6,000 a year in savings from the duplex, plus her $2,700 a year in cash flow from the house, Tracy now has over **$26,000** in Rent Estate cash to invest after seven years. So now she buys another rental property: a single-family rental for $125,000.

This home provides about $550 a month in cash flow, or nearly **$4,000** a year after expenses—which, of course, Tracy adds to her REAF.

Year 8: Fourth Purchase

Now that Tracy has a solid Rent Estate track record, she sets her sights on another property. And this time, she's able to structure a deal that requires **no cash outlay** whatsoever. First she finds a duplex in need of repair. It costs $165,000, but Tracy finances the entire purchase—plus another $20,000 for renovations— using a hard-money lender. (We'll talk more about these private, nonbank lenders in the next chapter). The interest rate is higher, but the loan is easier to get, and Tracy knows how to make it work to her advantage.

The renovations are done in six months, and the property is now worth nearly $250,000. Tracy now refinances the property using a traditional 30-year mortgage with a bank. The private lender is paid off, with interest. And after Tracy's property management company finds her some excellent renters, the cash flow on this property brings in another **$4,000+** a year to invest.

All that, and it cost her *nothing*.

Year 9: Fifth Purchase

The next year, Tracy does the same thing: She buys another duplex in need of repair for about the same price. She finances it first through a private hard-money lender. She renovates it. Then she refinances it through a traditional bank. Add another **$4,000+** a year in cash flow—again, for a cash outlay of **$0**.

Year 10: Sixth Purchase

Tracy easily now has over **$50,000** to put toward a down payment on a new property, so she finds a triplex for $250,000. Once the tenants are in, she's clearing another almost **$5,000** a year in cash flow. And now, she decides to stop and take stock of where she's at.

In just 10 years, starting with just $5,000, Tracy now has six properties with a total of 11 rental units. And guess what? That first duplex is now worth **$194,000**, and the first home she bought is worth about **$100,000**.[1] That means the appreciation on those two properties alone is already over **$61,000**.

Even if Tracy does nothing for the next 20 years except save her cash flow in an investment account, this is what she'll end up with:[2]

- **$2.1 million worth of property**
- **$36,000 a year in annual cash flow**
- **$1 million in the bank**

If Tracy continues to earn 4 percent on her money in the bank (which is the usual retirement assumption), and she also earns her $36,000 a year in cash flow, she'll be making **$76,000** a year without ever running out of money. In fact, that money will grow with inflation.

THE SKEPTIC SPEAKS

"Are these numbers realistic? I mean, aren't you leaving something out?"

I'm confident in Tracy's numbers for a good reason: Her story closely mirrors my own. I've lived this example. But you're right, I am leaving something out. Because these numbers don't even reflect the fact that some of Tracy's properties will be paid off at different times. When this happens, she'll get to keep *all* the rent

---

1   Assumes a 3.5% appreciation rate.

2   Assumes property appreciation of 3.5% and 4.5% rent growth every three years.

money without having to pay off a mortgage. This will make her cash flow explode. So actually, the numbers are a little conservative.

What the numbers don't reflect is the highly rewarding personal side of the equation. Along the way, Tracy has helped her tenants: young families, single moms and dads, people going through major life transitions, others seeking to repair their credit. Plus, by renovating properties, she's improved neighborhoods and raised the property values for the people who live in them. Nobody has lost in this scenario, and lots of people have won—especially Tracy.

Let's dive into the details on how you can be like Tracy and build your Rent Estate Empire.

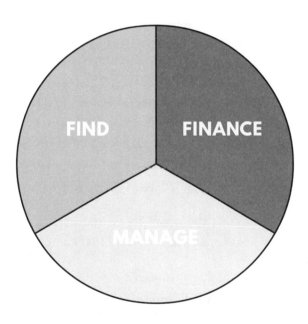

Find, Finance, Manage

Once you buy your first rental property—once you get it cash-flowing, see the money landing in your bank account every month, and look with amazement at your tax savings every April—you'll find that Rent Estate is like those old potato chip commercials: It's hard to stop at just one. (If Rent Estate isn't a legal drug, then I don't know what is.)

The truth is, adding to your Rent Estate portfolio is a lot easier than you might think. In fact, most Rent Estate investors are regular folks who own up to five properties. That's because multiplying your Rent Estate properties *doesn't* multiply your financial and time commitments—if you do it right.

I learned this firsthand after I acquired my Phoenix duplex in college. Once I experienced what it was like to live rent-free while owning an appreciating asset (with growing equity funded by somebody else), how could I resist the urge for more? As I mentioned in the introduction, I still own that duplex—plus 13 other Rent Estate properties. If you do the math, it's obvious that I haven't gone crazy and bought a new property every week; more like an average of one a year. And every time, I've done my homework, acted in a meticulous way before pulling the trigger, and outsourced.

Each of my properties has the ability to deliver the Four Pillars of Financial Freedom: long-term cash flow, equity, appreciation, and tax breaks. They also deliver peace of mind, because they provide financial security for my wife, Tiffany, and me—including a college fund for our kids and an additional retirement revenue stream.

The key to flinging open the doors to financial freedom is moving beyond your first Rent Estate property, and that comes down to three repeatable processes:

1. Finding additional rental properties.
2. Securing the financing to buy them.
3. Setting up the ongoing management to keep them running smoothly.

Find, Finance, Manage. Rent Estate isn't Rent Estate unless it covers all three, and you can't realize its full benefits unless you tap outside resources for all of them. Let's look at each one and see how we can make them as easy as possible.

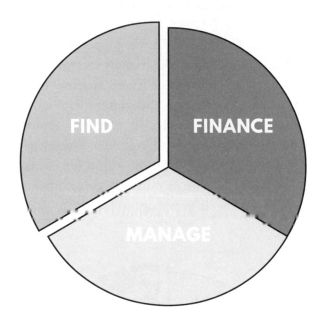

Finding More Properties

You can apply many of the same techniques you used to find your first Rent Estate property to your second, thirteenth, or thirtieth. Any Rent Estate property you buy should deliver the Four Pillars of long-term cash flow, equity, appreciation, and tax breaks. That never changes.

If your first investment property was the home you used to live in, then keep looking for other properties in the same neighborhood. That's the path of least resistance, and it's also just plain smart. But if you started from scratch in finding your first property, then you should continue working with a Rent Estate–savvy real estate agent and participating in your local investment real estate clubs.

If you want to do some detective work on your own, you can tap online resources like Trulia.com that specialize in finding residential real estate opportunities. Also take a look at realtor.com, the official website of the National Association of Realtors. For opportunities in the market of "troubled" (and undervalued) homes, realtytrac.com and auction.com are both worth exploring.

Online resources for finding Rent Estate property are getting better, more comprehensive, and more user-friendly every day. We're rapidly approaching a world in which Rent Estate investors can find excellent rental properties anywhere in the country without even setting foot inside of them. Imagine a series of competing apps that use big data and hands-on expertise to send you Rent Estate leads based on your specific criteria. There's no reason why a Rent Estate investor in Cleveland shouldn't be able to purchase a single-family rental in Austin without ever seeing it in person. In fact, we're already there.

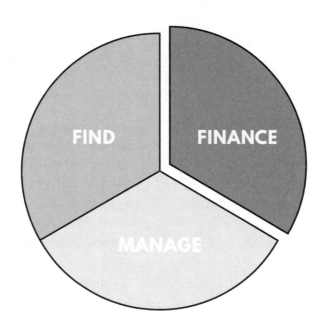

Financing More Properties

The financing part of Rent Estate is something I'm particularly passionate about, because I think *leverage* is one of the world's best-kept secrets. It's also the single most important element to master if you want to build a highly profitable Rent Estate portfolio.

Most people don't fully understand the concept of leverage, so I define leverage in a very simple way:

> **Leverage is using other people's money**
> **to make more of your own.**

If you have a mortgage, then you're already using leverage: You're borrowing money from a bank to buy a large asset (your home) with the assumption that the interest you're paying will be eclipsed by its equity and rising values over time. Unless you have millions of dollars in cash lying around, building your Rent Estate Empire requires leverage. In fact, even if you *did* have that kind of cash, using other people's money is still the smarter way to go.[3]

Here, I'd like to focus on four important aspects of leveraged financing: 1) using third-party lenders who specialize in Rent Estate transactions; 2) tapping the benefits of FHA loans; 3) using hard-money lenders, especially to buy properties in need of repair; and 4) 1031 exchanges.

Third-Party Private Lenders

I've mentioned that it's relatively easy to get a traditional bank to lend you money to buy rental property. It's certainly easier than getting a loan for any other kind of investment. But in the last few years, a new breed of lenders has also entered the marketplace—institutions that focus on the needs of residential real estate investors and provide loans for single-family rental properties.

JOINING THE RENT
ESTATE REVOLUTION

---

3 Keep in mind that leverage isn't without risk, especially when it comes to loans that involve what's known as a "personal guarantee." If your mortgage or loan agreement includes a personal guarantee, then know that your lender can go after your personal assets if they don't make their money back.

The potential advantage of working with these new lenders is that they "get" Rent Estate. In addition to offering fixed rates (which are essential), they can also offer benefits like:

- Fast-tracking loans, so you can close more quickly than with a traditional bank.

- A national footprint that enables you to obtain a loan for property anywhere in the country, instead of just in your local market.

- The ability to refinance a current Rent Estate mortgage or tap the equity in your existing properties.

- A line of credit to help you acquire additional properties and build your Rent Estate portfolio.

I encourage you to do your own research on these providers, but it's easy to see why going with a specialized, Rent Estate–friendly lender might provide more benefits than a traditional bank.

FHA Loans

I touched on FHA loans in Chapter 8 and in the Tracy example, and now I'd like to provide some more detail. To recap, an FHA loan is a mortgage that's offered by a private lender and insured by the Federal Housing Administration.[4] These loans go back almost a century, and their bottom-line advantage is that they generally involve less rigorous lending standards and lower down payments for the consumer. In other words, they require less of your own money and more of somebody else's (can you say "leverage"?).

Single-family homes and two- to four-unit buildings all qualify for FHA loans, provided they're in decent shape, they aren't too expensive, and you reside in the property. The U.S. Department of Housing and Urban Development (HUD) sets FHA loan limits annually, and they vary by area and property values. By

---

4   Note: The FHA is an insurer, not a lender. If you look at FHA loans through different approved lenders, don't be surprised if their interest rates vary somewhat.

way of comparison, the current FHA loan limit for a single-family home in Stamford, Connecticut, is $601,450, but in St. Paul, Minnesota, it's $332,350.[5]

The key factor in determining your down payment on an FHA loan is your credit rating. For example, if you have a credit score of 580 or higher, then you can get an FHA mortgage for a down payment as low as 3.5 percent of the home's purchase price (as of this writing). If your score is between 500 and 579, then you'll need a down payment of at least 10 percent. And if you're lower than that, then chances are you won't qualify. Also, you must live in the building for a specified amount of time.

Other advantages of FHA-insured loans include the following:

- If you can't (or don't want to) tap your own resources for a down payment, you can use a gift from a family member or a grant from a state or local government down payment assistance program.
- The FHA allows home sellers, builders, and lenders to pay some of the borrower's closing costs, such as appraisals, credit reports, and title expenses.
- If you're eyeing a property that needs repairs, then you can secure a special FHA loan product called a 203(k). The advantage here is that the loan amount is based on the *projected value* of the property after you do the repairs, rather than its current value. You can actually finance up to $35,000 in painting, cabinet replacement, new fixtures, and other nonstructural repairs.

The catch on FHA loans (of course there's a catch) is that they require two kinds of mortgage insurance to protect the lender from default. The first was recently cut from 0.85 percent of the

5   U.S. Department of Housing and Urban Development, "FHA Mortgage Limits," March 16, 2017, https://entp.hud.gov/idapp/html/hicostlook.cfm.

loan amount to 0.60 percent[6], and you can either pay it up front or have it folded into the mortgage. The second one is based on the loan amount, the loan length, and essentially the size of your down payment. This one you pay as a monthly premium.

Even with the mortgage insurance requirement, FHA-insurance financing can be the best way to buy your first Rent Estate property.

Hard-Money Lenders

Hard-money lending was also touched on in the Tracy example—and deliberately so, because it's an excellent Rent Estate resource for people who don't have mountains of cash lying around.

A soft-money lender is a traditional bank or mortgage lender. You put some money down, you borrow the cost of the home, and you pay the loan back over a long period of time, usually at a relatively low interest rate. Hard-money lenders are called that simply because the loan you receive is made against a hard asset—the home. (When you think about it, this really isn't any different from the way a bank treats a home loan, so the distinction is a little strange.)

Some people have a misperception about hard-money lenders and assume that they all report to Tony Soprano. Not true. Many individuals and businesses use hard-money loans all the time, not just in real estate but also for equipment purchases and other capital-intensive business investments. I've used hard-money lenders plenty of times, and they're solid, legitimate businesses.

The real difference between soft- and hard-money lenders is that because hard-money lenders aren't banks, they don't have to deal with the same level of regulation and bureaucracy.

6   Gail MarksJarvis, "FHA Cuts Insurance Premiums on Mortgages, Saving Average Borrower Hundreds," *Chicago Tribune*, January 9, 2017, http://www.chicagotribune.com/business/ct-fha-lowers-mortgage-premiums-0110-20170109-story.html.

This means you can often get all the money you need to buy a property, quickly, with no money down and no application fees. The potential downside is that you'll pay a higher interest rate—often 12–18 percent—which is why these loans are often used in buy-and-flip transactions.

So why are hard-money loans attractive in the world of Rent Estate? Simple: They're quick and easy to secure, and you can sometimes borrow *more* than the value of the property. That means if you're looking at a fixer-upper (say, a duplex in need of repairs), you can potentially finance 100 percent of the building *plus* 100 percent of the repair costs. Rather than "buy and flip," this is "fix and hold."

As we saw with Tracy, the beauty of hard-money, fix-and-hold transactions is that you can use hard money to quickly buy and improve a property, then refinance the property using a traditional soft-money loan. This gives you the best of all worlds: speed, improvements, bang for the buck, low long-term interest rates, and *leverage.* Hard-to-soft financing is a smart way to add to your Rent Estate portfolio and maximize the value of your investments, and I've used it many times myself.

1031 Exchanges

They may not have a sexy name, but 1031 exchanges are a potentially useful tool. They basically grease the wheels and take some friction out of the system—a rarity when it comes to our federal tax code.

Basically, a 1031 exchange allows you to swap one business or investment asset for another without being taxed. The law isn't strictly limited to real estate, but as it applies to Rent Estate, a 1031 exchange means that as the value of one Rent Estate property increases, you can roll that gain over into the down payment on another property when you sell the first one, without being taxed in the process.

But keep in mind, Rent Estate isn't about buying and selling; it's about buying, holding, and renting out. So while a 1031 exchange can be useful when you do decide to sell one of your rental properties, it shouldn't be something you use too often. Also, because the tax code is always full of nuances and exceptions, always work with a CPA or other tax professional before you use a 1031.

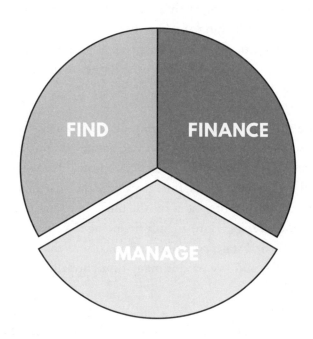

Managing More Properties

In the introduction, I described those scrappy days when I opened the Renters Warehouse Phoenix office. This was my baptism by fire into the world of big-time property management, and it's forever burned in my brain.

Before we figured out a better way to do things, my business partner and I would spend day after day driving all over Phoenix—collecting a late rent payment here, fixing a cabinet there. Here an inspection, there an eviction, everywhere a home showing. Not knowing any better, we would pass each other multiple times while driving through the city trying to keep up with the workload.

Looking back, it took far too long for us to dedicate ourselves to specific areas of the city (when we finally did, we each probably saved $300 a month on gas). As we grew, we were also able to implement the full Renters Warehouse model and assign individual staff to specific areas of property management. It takes one set of skills to collect rent; it takes an entirely different set to find high-quality tenants, or secure competitive bids on maintenance and repair work.

At the same time, we continued to pioneer technology that made property management more efficient and cost-effective for us—and more convenient, transparent, and user-friendly for our clients.

This brings me to the single most critical factor in growing your Rent Estate Empire:

**Your ability to purchase additional properties
depends on having a professional
property manager on your side.**

You can outsource finding and financing Rent Estate properties, but unless you also leave the management to someone else, you'll destroy your ability to grow your Rent Estate portfolio. And that's not "freedom."

Rent Estate Rockstar J.D. Dickerson learned this the hard way. With over 20 properties under his belt, he tried to manage everything himself while also working his day job, and the stress took over his life. He was convinced that no one in the world could manage his properties better than he could, until his wife finally convinced him to outsource the headache. Today, he still does, and here's why:

- J.D. realized that he could actually live off the cash flow generated by his properties *right now*.

- He quickly learned that outsourcing property management was more than worth the cost, especially when measured against the extra time he got to spend with his young family.

- He reluctantly acknowledged that we actually did a better job than he had done on his own. (Tough to admit for a proud DIYer.)

Property management now combines technology and human expertise to make outsourcing Rent Estate property management so easy, effective, and affordable for you, there's simply no reason to DIY anymore. In fact, if I didn't feel confident that the property management piece of Rent Estate was 100 percent ready for prime time, then I wouldn't be writing this book. Thankfully, it is. And that's the heart of why Rent Estate is finally ready to take off as an investment tool for the average Joe or Jane.

When you think about property management, think of it as more than just collecting the rent. It encompasses all of the elements of Rent Estate that aren't directly related to finding and financing property. And just as we've talked about the Four Pillars of Financial Freedom, think of these *Four Pillars of Property Management Freedom:*

1. The Freedom to Outsource Number Crunching

Do you have a magical "big data" machine to figure out the exact right amount to charge in rent for your properties? No, but others do. So why not take advantage of it?

2. The Freedom to Outsource Tenant Placement

Do you have the time to play "Renters Roulette" and spend hours of your time advertising your property, poring through tenant applications, and handling property inspections? No, so why not let someone else do it?

3. The Freedom to Outsource Rent Collection and Maintenance Coordination

Do you enjoy making phone calls asking for money, and spending hours on the phone getting estimates from plumbers and electricians? If you do, then I might have a job for you at Renters Warehouse. If you don't, then why not turn it over to someone else?

4. The Freedom to Not Worry about the Unexpected

Do you revel in the possibility of having to deal with property-ownership curveballs like accidental tenant damage and pesky eviction costs? No, so why not take advantage of property management services that can mitigate your risks and save you hundreds of thousands of dollars?

I think you have a right to all of these freedoms—because ultimately, they all add up to your *financial* freedom. But can you find a property management firm that can help you achieve those freedoms? Not all firms are created equal. So when you decide to form that all-important property-management partnership, keep a checklist in mind.

8 THINGS TO LOOK FOR IN A PROPERTY MANAGEMENT FIRM

1. They charge you a flat monthly fee instead of a percentage of the rent.
2. They have separate teams of specialists to handle things like tenant placement and maintenance requests.
3. They offer a warranty on tenants they place.
4. They offer an eviction service, but also have a very low tenant eviction rate.
5. They have a proven track record (backed by real data) in finding high-quality tenants quickly.
6. They can handle rent collection electronically and transfer funds directly to your bank account.
7. They handle most legal paperwork and red tape.
8. Their service includes providing you with monthly accounting statements and other financial reports.

A Vision of the Very Near Future

Now that I've laid out the elements of building your Rent Estate Empire, I want to leave you with the ultimate vision of how Rent Estate is going to work for you. This is a world in which Rent Estate plays a vital role in your investment portfolio, and where you can outsource virtually everything related to it, build a national portfolio with minimal time and risk, and make it all as profitable as possible.

Imagine a world in the very near future in which:

- You have an app on your phone that always knows exactly what you're looking for in residential real estate and consistently funnels prospective Rent Estate properties your way—not just in your hometown, but all over the country.

- When you find a home you want to buy, your trusty Rent Estate financial firm (which already gave you the loans on your first three properties) approves a mortgage on the new one nearly overnight.

- Your property management partner has already determined the rent you can charge (which helped you figure out whether or not to buy the property). Now that you own it, they step in to find great tenants and handle the ongoing grunt work of maintenance, repair, and red tape—all while you sit back and watch the cash roll in.

- That property manager develops a system in which you can divert some of your monthly cash flow into an account to fund future Rent Estate purchases.

Sound like a fantasy scenario? It's not. In fact, J.D. Dickerson is basically there. He retired from his day job, but he still does Rent Estate—knowing that at any time, he can buy a property in Houston while sipping on a margarita in Islamorada, Florida. He's still involved in all key decisions, and he maintains a personal connection to his tenants. But he also gets to sit back, count his money, and catch tonight's dinner. And that's *his* American Dream.

RENT ESTATE RECAP

Rent Estate isn't about owning just one rental property; it's about having several. *That's* what truly opens the doors to financial freedom. And that requires you to know how to find, finance, and manage multiple properties. Luckily, it's never been easier to do all three. Human and technological resources can locate high-quality Rent Estate properties. Traditional banks and specialty lenders can make financing more accessible than ever before. And property management has graduated from a world dominated by mom-and-pop outfits to a highly professional (and highly affordable) industry.

---

3 TAKEAWAYS

1. The only way to achieve financial freedom through Rent Estate is through *volume*, or owning multiple properties.

2. If you don't outsource key elements of finding, financing, and managing your properties, then you'll eventually hit a ceiling in the number of properties you can have, the financial benefits you can realize, and the personal freedom you can enjoy.

3. Hiring a professional property management firm to handle everything from rent collection to evictions frees you to concentrate on growing your Rent Estate portfolio instead of managing your properties.

ACTION ITEM

Check out our complete list of quality third-party partners for finding and financing Rent Estate properties at RentEstateRevolution.com.

SECTION 3

SUMMARY

Joining the Rent Estate Revolution has never been easier. It comes down to choosing the right first investment property, understanding the numbers and financial terminology, and knowing how to repeat the process to grow your Rent Estate Empire profitably.

If you already own a home, then your first rental property might be right under your nose—especially once you determine what you can charge in rent and do the *real* math on whether renting will ultimately deliver more value than a one-and-done sale. If you don't own a home, then locating your first property starts with finding a Rent Estate–savvy real estate agent to advise you.

When it comes to the financial side of Rent Estate, you need to understand the big stuff and the small stuff. The fact is, Rent Estate is built to potentially out-perform savings accounts, stocks, and other investments when it comes to stability, consistency of returns, accessibility, inflation, and tax advantages. But to gauge the potential return of any *individual* Rent Estate property, you need to calculate its cash-on-cash return and see how it might perform over the long term.

Finally, growing your Rent Estate Empire essentially involves successfully repeating three processes:

1. Finding additional properties using other people's research.
2. Financing them using other people's money.
3. Managing them using other people's time and expertise.

Excellent third-party resources now exist on all three of these fronts, but it's the *management* side that really makes Rent Estate "doable" for regular people. For a relatively low investment, you can now outsource nearly every aspect of Rent Estate to professionals—and spend your time managing your money instead of managing your properties.

CONCLUSION

The Rent Estate Revolution is the New American Dream.
It's changing homeownership. It's changing real estate. It's changing retirement. It's changing investing.

People have long known the financial power of buying and renting out single-family homes. But today, renting has kicked into a higher gear that—like a certain other Revolution—is driven by the unquenchable thirst for independence.

Americans love the freedom of not being tied down to a mortgage. Property owners love the freedom of outsourcing their headaches. And the missing piece to greater freedom is finally in place for all: Residential property management has become so comprehensive, so affordable, so efficient, and so national in scope that there's virtually no limit to the number of properties you can own, manage, and cash in on.

- **Rent Estate is the new real estate.** Instead of "buying and flipping" properties, more Americans are "buying and holding," because Rent Estate delivers all the benefits of real estate investments—and then some.

- **Rent Estate is an amazing way to leverage leverage.** Instead of wasting their own time and money, Americans are finding properties using other people's knowledge, financing them using other people's money, and managing them using other people's time.

- **Rent Estate is "real estate for the rest of us."** Instead of struggling to save up large amounts of capital, Americans are beginning their Rent Estate journeys with a few thousand dollars, and then growing their portfolios using only the cash generated by their Rent Estate investments.

- **Rent Estate is a win-win.** Instead of feeling like they're taking advantage of people and situations, Americans are using Rent Estate to help individuals and families find affordable housing, save money, repair their credit, and live where they want to live.

- **Rent Estate is retirement security.** Instead of relying solely on Social Security or 401(k)s, Americans are adding Rent Estate to their retirement portfolios and realizing the long-term cash flow, equity, appreciation, and tax benefits it's built to deliver.

Rent Estate changed my life. Every day, I feel the financial peace of mind it has brought to me and my family. Every day, I feel gratified for the connections I've made with my tenants along the way. And every day, I see how Rent Estate does the same thing for folks just like me.

So I have to ask: Have you bought your first Rent Estate property yet? If you want to open the doors to financial freedom; if you want to feel better about your kids' education and your retirement years; if you want to live the New American Dream—then take my advice: Think about everything you've just read. Digest the free resources at RentEstateRevolution.com. Then ask yourself one final question: *What am I waiting for?*

See you in the Revolution!

ABOUT THE AUTHOR

Kevin Ortner is the president and CEO of Minneapolis-based Renters Warehouse, the nation's largest and fastest-growing residential property management company. The son of a police officer who also dabbled in construction, Kevin learned about real estate from the ground up as a kid, using that knowledge to acquire his first property as a college freshman. Since then, he has grown his Rent Estate holdings to build retirement savings and fund educational investments for his family.

In 2015, Kevin was honored with both an American and International Stevie® Business Award for his achievements as Executive of the Year. Since he has taken the helm at Renters Warehouse, the company has secured elite Honor Roll status on the prestigious Inc. 500|5000 list of fastest-growing private companies in America for seven consecutive years. Passionate about youth mentorship and community, Kevin has been involved with the VANTAGE innovation program of the Minnetonka Public Schools since 2014, acting as a mentor and coach for young entrepreneurs.

Kevin lives in the Twin Cities with his wife, Tiffany, and their daughters, Macayla and Ainsley. His "why" in life is to help everyday Americans regain the lost American Dream of retirement security. This book is part of that mission.

RentersWarehouse®

America's #1 Rent Estate Company

Experts in Residential Leasing & Property Management

JOIN THE
RENT ESTATE REVOLUTION
TODAY!

- **Rent Estate Advising**

- **Free Home Rental Price Analysis**

- **Quality Tenant Placement in Just 17 Days on Average**

- **Free 6- to 18-Month Tenant Warranty**

- **Hundreds of Online Resources**

- **24/7 Property Management at Low, Flat-Rate Pricing**

- **National, Centralized, and Standardized Single-Family Rental Portfolio Services**

- **Local Market Staff and Expertise**

"Rent Estate is freedom. I get the financial benefits, Renters Warehouse handles the problems!"

—J.D. DICKERSON, Rent Estate Investor

RentersWarehouse.com · RentEstateRevolution.com